NOR
DELIGHTS

A Guide to the Hidden Joys
of the North of England

pocket mountains ltd

For Neil, Tommy and Danny –
still the best travelling companions

Published by
Pocket Mountains Ltd
Holm Street, Moffat, DG10 9EB
pocketmountains.com

ISBN: 978-1-907025-471

A catalogue record for this book is available
from the British Library

The author and publisher have made every
effort to ensure that the information in this
publication is accurate, and accept no
responsibility whatsoever for any loss, injury or
inconvenience experienced by any person or
persons whilst using this book.

Printed in Poland

CONTENTS

Another Place   6
Apollo Pavilion   9
Barter Books   12
The Beatles Shop   16
Beck Isle Museum of Rural Life   18
Brick Train   21
Carnforth Station   24
City Varieties Music Hall   26
The Comedy Carpet   29
Couple   32
Cumberland Pencil Museum   34
Fitzpatrick's Temperance
   Bar and Emporium   36
The Forbidden Corner   38
Forton Services   41
Grainger Market   43
Harbour Bar   46
Hat Works   49
Holy Island   51
Hornsea Museum   55
Ingrow Museum of Rail Travel   58
John Bull   63
Kielder Observatory   65
The Laurel and Hardy Museum   67
Levens Hall   70
The Lit & Phil   72
Marks in Time   76

Marsden Grotto   80
Middlesbrough Transporter Bridge   83
Midland Hotel   86
National Glass Centre   89
Peasholm Park   92
Piel Island   95
The Poison Garden   99
Pontefract Liquorice Festival   103
Port Sunlight   106
Preston Bus Station   110
The Rhubarb Triangle   114
Salford Lads Club   116
Saltburn-by-the-Sea
   Cliff Lift and Pier   120
The Scarborough Fair Collection   124
Shipley Glen Tramway   128
Spurn National Nature Reserve   131
Stott Park Bobbin Mill   134
They Shoot Horses, Don't They?   137
Threlkeld Quarry
   and Mining Museum   139
The Toast Rack   142
Tyne Pedestrian and Cyclist Tunnels   145
Whiteleys   148
Withernsea Lighthouse Museum   152
A World in Miniature   156

ACKNOWLEDGEMENTS

Thanks go to the owners, curators and custodians who have helped with this book. Firstly, for looking after and preserving their remarkable attractions; secondly, for patiently helping with the research. Special thanks to the following:

Tracy Cullen at The Alnwick Garden
Louise Bailey at Marks & Spencer Company Archive
Grace Dean at The City Varieties
Michael Trainor
Ann Clough at Whiteleys
Susie Bagot and family and Chris Crowder
at Levens Hall
Guilian Alonzi at The Harbour Bar
Leslie Holmes at Salford Lads Club
Sara Jo Harrison at the National Glass Centre
Richard Freeman at Shipley Glen Tramway
Jess Charlton at Yorkshire Wildlife Trust
Abbie McHolm at World in Miniature
John Wilson at prestonbusstation.co.uk
Guy and Gary at Kielder Observatory
Kay Easson at the Lit and Phil

Thanks also to Sarah Martin, Rosie Ferrier, Andy Huntington, Ally Payne, Greg Povey and Gareth Dobson who suggested Northern Delights to visit, and to everyone who has supported *Nothing To See Here*.

INTRODUCTION

Northern Delights is a follow-up to *Nothing To See Here: A Guide to the Hidden Joys of Scotland*, which was published by Pocket Mountains in 2011 to much acclaim.

The North of England has always been a fruitful hunting ground for lovers of the unusual. On numerous trips south (as The North is south when you're coming from Scotland) it has yielded many undersung delights like the Laurel and Hardy Museum in Ulverston, Cumbria's wonderful Piel Island or Preston's majestic Bus Station.

When it became clear that there were enough peculiar places to fill a book, family holidays became meticulously-planned expeditions to make sure that no stone was left unturned in the search for The North's hidden gems.

Defining 'The North' of England is a tricky business so the book's definition is geographical rather than spiritual, covering the counties of Northumberland, Durham, Cumbria, Yorkshire and Lancashire. Apologies to all Northerners south of that line.

Whichever way you look at it, The North is a wonderful place to visit.

ANOTHER PLACE CROSBY

Crosby beach has some strange visitors – 100 figures by *Angel of the North* creator Antony Gormley. Based on a cast of the artist's body, the sculptures are made out of cast iron and stand staring at the horizon. At first, on a busy day, they are hard to spot, arranged along 3km of shore and stretching almost 1km out to sea. At high tide just 10 or 15 can be seen, and only a few of them are visible from head to toe. The rest are partially submerged with some only head and shoulders above the water, not waving but drowning.

Up close the figures are worn by the elements, giving them a wonderful texture. Each one has a tag on its wrist with a number. Despite the fact that each figure is 650 kilos of high-grade British art they seem pretty approachable and local residents have adopted them as their own. They are sometimes adorned with sun-hats, motorbike helmets and even Santa outfits. They're also a handy place to leave your flip-flops if you're heading in for a paddle (but please, no swimming on this beach – it's too dangerous).

The statues weather the seasons, looking beautiful against a blue sky and steely against a cold, rainy winter's day. It's a unique spectacle, the figures in harmony with their surroundings – classic but elegant, random but orderly, anonymous but human. Amid the almost

endless comings and goings further out to sea, their solidity and stolidity bring an enormous sense of peace to the scene.

Initially part of a travelling exhibition, *Another Place* was only meant to be here for 16 months. It proved so popular that Sefton Council voted to keep it and now the iron incomers are a permanent part of the local landscape, standing strong as time and tide ebb and flow around them.

ACCESS AND OPENING TIMES

Crosby is just north of Liverpool – once you get near the town *Another Place* is well signposted. There is a car park at the beach, and it is also easy to reach by bus or rail. visitliverpool.com/things-to-do

APOLLO PAVILION PETERLEE

The Apollo Pavilion is a curious thing. Built between 1963 and 1970 in Peterlee, a new town in County Durham, it's an abstract concrete sculpture, plain white apart from two small murals decorating the upper deck. Designed to span a lake and link two sides of the Sunny Blunts housing estate, it has divided opinion ever since it was built.

At 25m wide, made from concrete cast on site, it's a hulking great brute, spectacularly out-of-scale to everything around it. Abstract artist Victor Pasmore was brought in to design it after modernist hero Berthold Lubetkin's high-rise ideas for Peterlee proved unsuitable. Pasmore wanted

'The Pivvy', as it is known locally, to 'lift the activity and psychology of an urban housing community onto a universal plane'. Aspirations were high, and it was named The Apollo Pavilion after the moon mission which was reaching for the stars around the same time.

Almost immediately it became a haven for ne'er-do-wells and teeny-tipplers. Over the next few years vandalism, council in-fighting and neglect left the pavilion in a sorry state. The murals faded, the concrete decayed and the lake emitted a powerful pong. Eventually the steps to the upper deck were demolished and it was left to rot. When

it was turned down for Grade II listing in 1998 its future looked bleak.

For all its detractors the pavilion has always had fans too. The Apollo Pavilion Community Association has encouraged its appreciation, and public support has grown gradually. In 2008, Heritage Lottery funding helped to repair and renew the pavilion in time for its 40th birthday. It was listed successfully in 2011.

Today, the reinstated staircase, repainted murals and dapper white surfaces make a world of difference. The view from the previously inaccessible top deck cleverly frames the estate from different perspectives, and it suddenly becomes clear that this was meant to be a place for reflecting and re-presenting the world immediately around it. It all makes sense when you stop to appreciate it.

ACCESS AND OPENING TIMES

The Apollo Pavilion is on Oakerside Drive, Peterlee, County Durham, SR8 1LE. From the A19 turn towards Peterlee, take the second right beside Our Lady of the Rosary Church into Passfield Way and Oakerside Drive is third on the left (signposted 'Pasmore's Apollo Pavilion'). Parking is signposted. Go downhill from the car park, past the flats and along the path. You can't miss it. apollopavilion.info

BARTER BOOKS

ALNWICK

Barter Books is one of Britain's largest second-hand bookshops, and some say the best. Alnwick's roomy Victorian station has been transformed into a temple for book-worshippers of all ages and persuasions. There are new books and old, popular paperbacks and cult classics, precious first editions and cut-price bargains – something for everyone.

As a homage to its station heritage the trains remain, but now they are miniaturised and running on top of the many bookshelves. Instead of train lines, there are lines of poetry beautifully written and threaded over the shelves, watched over by a mural of famous writers. There are open fires and comfy chairs. On one wall, there is a neon sunrise and, underneath, bookshelves radiate out like the sun's rays. Customers orbit the bays like planets, floating in a galaxy of words.

Opened in 1991 by Mary Manley and her husband Stuart, the shop takes its name from the bartering system in place. Swap a bag of books for credit and find some new reading matter. With a playful children's area and an atmospheric café in the old waiting room, it's a wonder anyone ever leaves.

As well as being an impressive bookshop, Barter Books is the home of the recent Keep Calm and Carry On phenomenon. Originally designed as a motivational poster at the start of

13

World War II, the campaign wasn't used and the slogan was lost until the owners found an original poster in a box of books. Reproductions sold like hot cakes and soon the slogan covered everything from mugs to wallpaper. There is always the feeling that another gem is lurking here, so visit soon to see what you can find.

ACCESS AND OPENING TIMES

Barter Books is at Alnwick Station, Wagon Way Road, Alnwick, Northumberland NE66 2NP. The shop is open daily in summer 9am-7pm and in winter 9am-5pm (Saturdays 7pm). barterbooks.co.uk

THE BEATLES SHOP LIVERPOOL

The Beatles Shop is the original and best place to stock up on your Fab Four memorabilia. Opened in 1984 it has been slowly eclipsed by bigger, brighter, more modern Beatles emporia – none of which have an ounce of its charm and authenticity.

Situated in a basement on Mathew Street just like the Cavern Club where it all began, it is small and dark and hugely atmospheric. Layers and layers of Beatles memories and memorabilia cover the walls from the Beatles carpet right up to the ceiling. Vintage souvenirs, official and unofficial, mingle with fan letters and collectors' pieces, as life-size cardboard cutout Beatles look on.

The higgledy-piggledy charm of the stock, combined with the steady stream of Beatles fans, makes it feel like a place of pilgrimage rather than a souvenir shop. The eternally good-humoured proprietor is always ready to talk about music and happily hands fans a pen to sign the pillar or a stick of Beatles rock to take away. The wall of fame shows

celebrated stars who have visited, including Beatle Ringo Starr, who popped in for a look around in 1992.

The shop sells something for every purse, from Beatles badges and pencils to gold discs and guitars. All Beatles are treated equally, and every era is represented. There is no judgement on what has aged well and what hasn't – from moptops to moustaches, Sgt Pepper to solo albums it's all here.

In the 30 years since the shop opened the Beatles industry in Liverpool has mushroomed. Although other Beatles shops are available, this is the one that feels most closely connected to the band and the music. If you like the Beatles it's a must, and even if you don't, it's worth popping in to see a little piece of Fab Four fandom.

ACCESS AND OPENING TIMES

The Beatles Shop is on 31 Mathew Street, Liverpool, L2 6RE. It is open Mon-Sat 9.30am-5.30pm, Sun 10.30am-4.30pm. thebeatleshop.co.uk

BECK ISLE MUSEUM OF RURAL LIFE PICKERING

Beck Isle Museum is a very local museum, displaying scenes from everyday life in this small corner of Pickering, North Yorkshire. By collecting the sort of objects that used to be common but are now old-fashioned, it manages to be familiar and exotic at the same time.

Some 27 themed rooms, spread over the interior and courtyard of an old doctor's surgery, show life as it once was. The Victorian parlour is stuffed with birds, bibles and embroidery – no TV, of course, and no computers in the print studio, where local papers and posters are typeset by hand.

The Sydney Smith room is particularly successful in capturing times past. Smith was a local photographer who documented the people and places of Ryedale from 1900 to 1956. His fantastic archive of photos and camera equipment complements the rest of the museum, helping the visitor to gain an insight into who might have lived in a house like this.

Looking back in time, it's interesting to see good things lost and other not-so-good things happily banished. The chemist's, evocative as it is with its pep pills and colourful carboys, is mildly

terrifying, showing how far medicine has come. The pub next door is a good place to ponder the march of progress over a game of shove ha'penny, before admiring the Rolls Royce razor blades in the barber's. Fashion aficionados can enjoy the retro outfits in the village shop and dress up in the gentlemen's outfitter's, with its starched collars and bow ties.

Outside the house, the displays move on to farming, forestry, bee-keeping and broom-making – all essential activities at one point. The wheelwright's and blacksmith's rooms lead towards more opportunities for horseplay in the old schoolroom.

Recommending somewhere for its ordinariness may sound like a backhanded compliment, but Beck Isle Museum does it beautifully, elevating everyday life to something quite extraordinary.

ACCESS AND OPENING TIMES
The museum is on Beck Isle in the centre of Pickering, North Yorkshire, YO18 8DU. It is open daily from February to November 10am-5pm.
beckislemuseum.org.uk

Winnowing Machine to remove the chaff from the wheat.

BRICK TRAIN

DARLINGTON

As you travel along the A66 on the edge of Darlington you'll see a train on one side of the road. Nothing unusual in that, except this one isn't going anywhere. Designed by leading contemporary artist and sculptor David Mach, *Train* is made from 185,000 local 'Accrington Nori' bricks and commemorates Darlington's illustrious heritage as 'home of the railways'.

The Stockton-Darlington Railway, which opened in 1825, was Britain's first permanent steam locomotive railway. So at 60m long and 6m high, it is a perfect rendering of the 1938 classic locomotive 'Mallard', complete with plume of billowing smoke.

Mach describes his train as being 'as much a piece of architecture as a sculpture'. Creating a large-scale, lifelike whole out of thousands of commonplace objects is his trademark. Apart from *Train* he has made a number of artworks worldwide, such as *The Temple at Tyre* from car tyres in Edinburgh and his *Big Heids* from steel

piping beside the M8 in Lanarkshire. He puts his interest in mass-production down to a job in a bottling plant he had as a young man back home in Fife. But even though the constituent parts may be common, the end result is far from throwaway and his work is usually thoughtfully designed and painstakingly constructed with sensitivity to the local area and its long-term future. The sculpture includes 20 special 'bat' bricks to encourage these protected nocturnal creatures to nest there.

As with many public art projects it has its opponents, with critics suggesting the money could have been put to better use elsewhere. However, from a distance it brightens up an otherwise featureless journey along the A66 and close-up you can't help but marvel at the mind-boggling detail that has gone into it.

ACCESS AND OPENING TIMES

Train sits next to Morrisons at Morton Park Industrial Estate, Yarm Road, about midway between Darlington town centre and Teesside Airport – it is AA signposted. davidmach.com

CARNFORTH STATION

Carnforth Station may not stand out as you whizz through it on the train, but for some it is the most romantic of all stations, following its starring role in David Lean's classic 1945 film *Brief Encounter*.

Set in 1938 in the fictional small town of Milford, Laura Jesson (Celia Johnson) and Alec Harvey (Trevor Howard) meet in the station's Refreshment Room after a passing train sends grit into Laura's eye. Alec (a doctor) removes it in a chivalrous manner and soon their friendship develops into romance. The station plays a vital supporting role, with the clock symbolising the pressure of time and the passing trains creating a steamy atmosphere that builds to a climactic point.

The film was based on a Noel Coward play called *Still Life*, set entirely in a station tearoom, so finding the right location was key. When it wasn't possible to film in London because of the wartime blackout, location scouts found Carnforth – it was big enough to act as a mainline station and northern enough to avoid lighting restrictions for filming at night. The platforms were far enough apart to introduce the jeopardy of almost-missed trains while the long ramps meant that no one clattered

down steps to catch them. It was perfect.

Today, the station still gives off an impressive vintage air. The buildings have been refurbished and opened in 2003 as the Carnforth Station Heritage Centre. Inside, tightly packed displays on *Brief Encounter* (including the film permanently playing in a small cinema area), trains and the local area keep visitors of all ages amused. The Brief Encounter Refreshment Room has been refitted in 1940's style with a big steamy urn, home baking and generous teapots to cry into, if need be.

There are regular events such as 1940s nights and live jazz bands to really get in the mood, and occasional steam days. Its well-preserved features and unique cinema heritage make Carnforth Station ideal for a fleeting trip or, even better, a lingering encounter.

ACCESS AND OPENING TIMES
The Heritage Centre is on Warton Road, Carnforth, Lancashire, LA5 9TR and is open daily from 10am to 4pm. The Refreshment Room is open daily, 9am to 4pm. carnforthstation.co.uk

CITY VARIETIES MUSIC HALL LEEDS

The City Varieties is one of only four surviving original Victorian music halls in the UK. Its showbiz roots go back to 1766 when the neighbouring White Swan Inn needed a 'Singing Room'.

The current building was opened in 1865 by proprietor Charles Thornton (also responsible for nearby Thornton's Arcade), and started life as Thornton's New Music Hall and Fashionable Lounge before becoming the Stansfield Varieties and later the City Palace of Varieties.

Its beautiful Victorian interior has been carefully conserved, all red velvet and gold leaf, with three floors and 'ashtrays' (private boxes) at the side for the toffs. It's hard to picture it now as it used to be – a bawdy place, crammed so full with 2000 people that you couldn't see the stage for smoke or hear the acts for the noise of the crowd.

It was always designed to deliver popular, affordable entertainment, in contrast to its sister venue, the Grand Theatre, also still going strong – the saying used to be 'wear your flat cap to the City Varieties and your top hat to the Grand Theatre'.

Famous names like Lily Langtry, Harry Houdini and Charlie Chaplin (who was paid £1 per week) all took the stage here, along with variety acts such as trapeze artists and cannon ball jugglers.

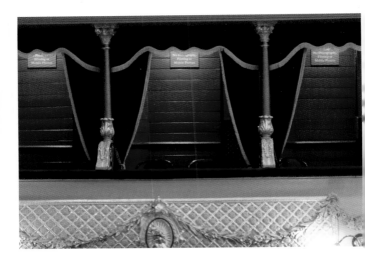

The 1950s turned decidedly seedy with striptease and burlesque shows, until the new owners decided to make it more family friendly. Now the calendar is full year round with pantomimes, comedians, and bands of all kinds.

Its most famous offering, *The Good Old Days*, was broadcast on the BBC for 30 years from 1953 to 1983. A recreation of proper Victorian-Edwardian music hall, it was known for the amazing alliterative descriptions by host Leonard Sachs, and roof-raising renditions of *Down At The Old Bull and Bush*. Today it runs twice a year with a slew of old-time comedians, singers and variety acts. Audience members are encouraged to dress up, so if you do go along there's almost as much to see in the stalls as there is on the stage.

A visit to the City Varieties is a tantalising taste of Victorian splendour. At the interval even the orange squash in the Circle Bar comes in a decanter. Treat yourself to a night out or look for the tours that run throughout the year for a little glimpse of the theatrical past.

ACCESS AND OPENING TIMES
The City Varieties Music Hall is on Swan St, Leeds, LS1 6LW. Backstage tours can be pre-booked. cityvarieties.co.uk

THE COMEDY CARPET BLACKPOOL

Blackpool is a funny old place, where visitors flock for entertainment and laughs in its many theatres, piers and ballrooms. So it's fitting that a town built on comedy now has some built into it.

The Comedy Carpet celebrates Blackpool's comedy heritage with what has to be the funniest piece of public art in the UK. It is not technically-speaking, a carpet, but a 2200m^2 artwork featuring more than 1000 tattifilarious jokes and catchphrases spread out on the prom at the foot of Blackpool Tower.

More than 160,000 granite letters set into bright white concrete spell out lines from the best-loved comedians and comedy writers in the British Isles, all of

whom have one thing in common – they performed in Blackpool.

Commissioned by Blackpool Council as part of a huge seafront regeneration project, artist Gordon Young worked with design studio Why Not Associates to create it. The memorable lines, coupled with the beautiful design and typography (drawn from playbills and other archive material), make a perfect double act. The clever layout can be read from any direction and even enjoyed from the giddy heights of Blackpool Tower.

The selection is fantastically eclectic, with songs and sketches and jokes old and new. Less is more – the catchphrases are short and

unattributed, so part of the fun is remembering who said which punchline and the way they told 'em. Every generation can find a line to make them chuckle, from Flanagan and Allen to Dick and Dom. Every corner of Britain is represented, from Jethro to Wee Jimmy Krankie.

The loveliest thing about it is seeing friends and families shriek with laughter as they find a favourite catchphrase or explain a joke to a friend. It's the one place where everyone has stars in their eyes, and pointing and laughing is positively encouraged.

Opened in 2011 to rapturous applause, it won a variety of awards for art and typography. Designed to last 100 years, it should keep visitors laughing for a long time to come.

ACCESS AND OPENING TIMES

The Comedy Carpet is on the promenade at the foot of Blackpool Tower.
comedycarpet.co.uk

COUPLE NEWBIGGIN-BY-THE-SEA

Blank-faced couples silently staring at the horizon are a common sight around the British coast, so Newbiggin-by-the-Sea had one permanently installed.

Instead of sitting in a car with a thermos of tea, Newbiggin's emotionless pair stand on a steel platform 300m offshore. Their backs turned to the beach, they stare at the sea, together but slightly apart, thinking great thoughts or none at all – it's hard to tell. At high tide the platform disappears, leaving them standing on water, still unruffled.

The distance makes it hard to get a sense of scale. They may look small, but really they are far away – at 5m high, an average man would be up to mid-thigh level. Nicknamed Ebenezer and Florence (Ebb and Flo), there is a smaller version on the prom, gazing blankly at their waterborne doppelgangers.

Simply called *Couple*, the pair were designed by British sculptor Sean Henry, who is known for his outsize lifelike figures. Modelled on a real but unnamed couple, they started life as 15cm figures, made of clay cast in bronze and hand-painted. The logistical challenges of installing Britain's first permanent offshore sculpture included finding the right kind of maritime paint,

transporting the figures by road and boat, and timing the installation around the area's migrating bird population.

Commissioned as part of the redevelopment of Newbiggin Bay, they top off a breakwater, which was installed in 2007. Years of coastal erosion had seen the beach disappear, taking visitors and the town's sense of pride with it. The £10m regeneration project brought 500,000 tonnes of sand in from Skegness to make a new beach, with the breakwater constructed to stop the tide washing it away again.

A statement piece of public art was designed to turn the coastal renewal project into something wider – a cultural renaissance for a town in decline. The North East of England was already peppered with successful public art pieces like Antony Gormley's *Angel of the North*, Claes Oldenburg's *Bottle of Notes* in Middlesbrough and Juan Muñoz's enigmatic *Conversation Piece* at South Shields, so there was faith in the importance of art in the community. Their photos and likenesses now appear around the town, like local celebs, and they provide an interesting focal point for visitors who also enjoy a good old stare at the horizon.

ACCESS AND OPENING TIMES
Newbiggin is 24km north of Newcastle in the southeast of Northumberland. newbigginbay.co.uk

33

CUMBERLAND PENCIL MUSEUM KESWICK

The Cumberland Pencil Museum in Keswick is a big draw for visitors to the Lake District. Regularly voted one of Britain's oddest days out, it certainly is quirky, but also surprisingly good, with well-thought-out displays and unusual exhibits creating a colourful story of this classic writing implement.

Keswick's first pencil factory opened in 1832, thanks to the plentiful supply of graphite found 300 years earlier in nearby Borrowdale. It later became the Cumberland Pencil Company which still runs the museum today.

Enter through a graphite mine and find out how the lead gets into your pencil. The whole process is explained, from the cedar trees used to form the casings to the coloured 'cores' or 'strips' inside. The displays show that the art of making a pencil is more complicated than you might think. The science of colour and the difficulty in getting consistent shades across different batches is a feat in itself, involving a machine designed to simulate bright Florida sunshine – something that is hard to come by in Keswick.

Pencil-related enigmas are explained –

from the mysterious HB and F codes (to signify darkness and hardness) to the incredible story of the Secret Wartime Pencil. Advances in pencil technology are recorded – from propelling pencils to watercolour pencils for artists. And there are fun exhibits ranging from the world's largest coloured pencil to a special diamond-encrusted pencil sent to the Queen for her jubilee.

After all this, the beautiful Derwent and Lakeland pencil packs that can't help but catapult you back to childhood and a model of Tower Bridge made from pencils really make you wonder if there's anything you can't do with this versatile instrument. After a visit here, you can't fail to see the point of pencils!

ACCESS AND OPENING TIMES

The Pencil Museum is at Southey Works, Keswick, Cumbria, CA12 5NG. It is open daily 9.30am-5pm.
pencilmuseum.co.uk

FITZPATRICK'S TEMPERANCE BAR AND EMPORIUM RAWTENSTALL

Fitzpatrick's Temperance Bar in Rawtenstall, Lancashire is the only surviving original temperance bar in Britain. That is, a bar that doesn't serve alcohol.

Opened in 1890, Fitzpatrick's was a product of the temperance movement, which preached abstinence from alcohol. 'The demon drink' was seen as a threat to good Christian values, and the Temperance Society was formed to encourage sobriety. Founded in Preston, it had a strong foothold in the north of England, where the working classes enjoyed a good drink. With no restrictions on the sale of alcohol, every hour was happy hour.

Initially, steering clear of spirits was enough to get you membership, but after a while 'taking the pledge' came to mean no alcohol whatsoever. In fact, the word 'teetotal' is said to come from one member, who spoke with a stammer and said that nothing would do except 'tee-tee-total abstinence'.

In the early 20th century, temperance bars became the focal point of many communities, with locals gathering for a quick sarsaparilla as the Band of Hope children sang uplifting songs. The Fitzpatrick family were renowned herbalists and ran a chain of temperance bars throughout Lancashire. Malachi Fitzpatrick, the last in the family

line, ran the Rawtenstall bar for more than 50 years and lived to 90 years, his long and healthy life attributed to the tonics and potions he brewed in the shop.

Fitzpatrick's now has new owners, who have given the place a sympathetic refit. Visitors can continue to enjoy their award-winning home-made cordials such as sarsaparilla, dandelion & burdock and blood tonic (a lot nicer than it sounds). The original bar is a tremendous looking thing, almost organ-like with mysterious stops for cream soda and 'Wino' among others. The shelves are filled with jars containing ingredients such as comfrey and borage and, for the less adventurous, traditional boiled sweets and herbal remedies.

Vintage bits and pieces, ranging from phrenology busts to packets of Asepso antiseptic soap, litter the bar. Familiar brands like Vimto (invented in Manchester as Vim Tonic) and Eno's had their roots in places like this. In the supermarket they have a job competing against shiny new products, but here they're in a fusty yet very pleasant world of their own. Herbalists have had to weather the storm of fashion over the years, shunned as the domain of cranks, so it's heartwarming to find Fitzpatrick's in such rude health.

ACCESS AND OPENING TIMES
Fitzpatrick's is at 5 Bank Street, Rawtenstall, Rossendale, BB4 6QS – the end of the street where it curves back onto Bury Road near Asda. Parking on the main street is by disk.
mrfitzpatricks.com

THE FORBIDDEN CORNER COVERHAM

The Forbidden Corner is a bit of a mystery. Before you go, it's difficult to know what to expect, and after you've been it's difficult to explain what just happened.

One succinct description is that it is a modern folly or a collection of follies in one garden – mazes, castles, statues and water features, none of which serve a practical function. Everything is designed to amuse or delight.

There is deliberately no map or guide so the first puzzle is wondering where to start. A green man figure carved from a tree points towards a gaping stone mouth. Once you have navigated the

giant epiglottis and passed through its rear end, you're ready to begin your adventure.

The layout sends you round in circles, with weird twists and turns thrown in. Sometimes the question is how to get in – or how to get out. You can catch a glimpse of something through the foliage and spend ages trying to find it. In the end you need to keep your wits about you and go with the flow (either of people, of water or the garden itself), avoiding cats, mice and the very devil himself along the way. After passing through temples, grottoes, castles and gardens you not only lose your sense of

WATCH
WHERE
YOU'RE GOING!

39

direction, but all sense of place or time.

The sculptures, ironworks and buildings are all beautifully done. This is down to a fruitful collaboration between Colin Armstrong, the owner of the Tupgill Estate, and his architect friend Malcolm Tempest. They took inspiration from other gardens and follies worldwide to develop what was initially a private garden into a playground for curious individuals.

Since opening in 1994, there have been regular additions to the garden so it bears repeated visits. Although it's a family attraction, be aware that some parts may frighten small or sensitive children, and there are some areas where visitors will be squashed or soaked. For most people, it's all part of the fun.

ACCESS AND OPENING TIMES

The Forbidden Corner is in Tupgill Park Estate, Middleham, Leyburn, North Yorkshire, DL8 4T. Entry is by advance online or phone booking only. theforbiddencorner.co.uk

FORTON SERVICES M6

The distinctive space-age tower of Lancaster (Forton) Services has become a well-loved landmark on the M6 motorway. Its modern-retro design is like something out of *Thunderbirds*, suddenly appearing on the roadside. Designed to stand out, it is a symbol of a different age, when motorway services were not somewhere for an anonymous pit stop but a holiday destination in themselves.

Commissioned by Top Rank Motor Inns and designed by architects Bill Galloway

and Ray Anderson for TP Bennett, Forton Services opened in 1965, the second services to open on the M6 after Charnock Richard. At the time, Britain's motorway network was in its infancy, with the first section opening seven years earlier in nearby Preston. More than just roads, they were symbols of Britain's economic and cultural optimism, carriers of hope for a brighter future.

The tower's design represented the glamour of air travel made accessible by car. The 20m-wide hexagon, which

looks like a displaced air traffic control tower, was designed to jut above the landscape, attracting visitors from miles around. A covered bridge allowed access from either side of the carriageway so there was no reason not to pop in.

Officially called The Pennine Tower, it originally held a 120-seater fine dining restaurant – 'the epitome of style', according to the architects. The Ministry of Transport policy at the time was to put service stations 'in places where the motorway passed through pleasant rural scenery, so that their potential users might find them attractive and restful'.

The roof was a sundeck with views of the Lake District, the Pennines, Morecambe Bay and Blackpool (on a good day). Imagine! You could even send a Forton Services postcard home to impress your friends.

After a few years, when the high-class dining idea didn't take off, the restaurant became a trucking lounge. By 1989 the tower faced extensive modernisation to comply with health and safety regulations, and closed to the public. This didn't stop English Heritage listing it as architecturally significant in 2012.

Today, Forton Services (now known as Lancaster Service Area) is not somewhere you're likely to go for a day out, but it does brighten the journey, catering for the modern traveller inside its magnificent retro exterior.

ACCESS AND OPENING TIMES
Forton (Lancaster) Services is between Junctions 32 and 33 on the M6, about 11km south of Lancaster.
tpbennett.com

GRAINGER MARKET NEWCASTLE UPON TYNE

When Newcastle's Grainger Market opened in 1835 it was Europe's largest indoor market. Now Grade I listed, it is one of the few to survive, and it is still thriving, with more than 100 stalls selling everything from baby clothes to gravestones.

Designed by architect John Dobson and built by Richard Grainger, who brought so many graceful neoclassical buildings to Newcastle town centre, it hasn't changed too much over the years. The famous Weigh House, originally built to measure cuts of meat, now services shoppers, who queue to have their weight discreetly noted down. Elsewhere, the only original Marks and Spencer's Penny Bazaar is always busy, as it has been since it opened in 1895 following on from M&S's first stall in Leeds Kirkgate Market.

Originally designed in a grid formation containing butchers' stalls and an open plan area for fruit and veg, it now holds a wider variety of stalls. The *Are You Being Served?* theme tune

ELECTRICAL SUPPLIES

REPAIR SERVICE · SHAVERS · MIXERS · TOASTERS · IRONS · KETTLES · HAIRDRYERS · ETC.

LAMPS · SWITCHES · PLUGS · SOCKETS · BATTERIES · CABLES · FUSES ETC.

Remington

PHILIPS

could have been specially written for it – perfumery, stationery and leather goods, wigs and haberdashery, kitchenware and food.

It's refreshingly simple – The Shaver Centre, Bags of Bags and The Cheap Tab Shop sell exactly what they say on the sign. There is something here for everyone, whether it's bananas, beef or batteries.

A tightening of purse strings combined with a rising interest in gourmet food make this market the perfect place to find a new flavour or sniff out an ingredient at a reasonable price. It doesn't have the rough edges of some local markets or the pretensions of others. The pyramids of fruit and veg are

shiny and fresh, and there are butchers' stalls so beautiful that it would make a vegetarian weep. If you don't want to cook, pick up something tasty from one of the food stalls, or just wander and enjoy the hubbub. Whatever you're looking for, Grainger Market makes shopping a pleasure.

ACCESS AND OPENING TIMES

Grainger Market is in Newcastle city centre near Grey's Monument, with entrances on Grainger Street, Clayton Street, Nun Street and Nelson Street. It is open every day, except Sundays and public holidays, from 9am.
graingermarket.org.uk

HARBOUR BAR

SCARBOROUGH

Whatever the weather outside it's always sunny in the Harbour Bar, Scarborough's perfectly-preserved 1950's ice-cream parlour. Inside, it's a glorious confection of chrome and yellow formica, like a Banana Split brought to life.

These fashionable milk bars sprang up in towns and cities all over Britain from the 1940s onwards, until more modern fast-food establishments pushed them out of favour. Today, original examples are as rare as hen's teeth, making the

Harbour Bar's survival all the more remarkable. The eye-popping décor, chosen because it was cost-effective and hard-wearing, has really proved its worth, still looking fresh and fashionable today.

Perch on a high stool at the counter or go for a comfortable booth, under the signs extolling the health-giving properties of ice cream. Waitresses in bright yellow uniforms bustle around in front of a pyramid of bottled fruit –

a nod, according to the owners, 'to earlier years where fresh fruit was hard to come by'.

It's not the only nod to earlier, simpler days. In fact, very little has changed since it opened in 1945. The Alonzi family, who still run it today, know when they've got a good thing going. The menu is refreshingly short and sweet. In a glorious change from swanky modern cafes, there are only two types of coffee on offer – normal and decaf. However, there are three types of Horlicks and, if that wasn't enough, there's Ovaltine too – you'll be spoilt for choice! Bovril and Biscuits are also available for those with a savoury tooth – the northern alternative to cocktails and canapés.

Giulian Alonzi, a third-generation Italian ice-cream maker, still makes the award-winning ice cream in the model factory at the rear, ready to dish it up as Knickerbocker Glories, Ice Cream Floats or sundaes for every day of the week. There is something for every purse and palate, so no wonder the Harbour Bar attracts visitors young and old from near and far, come rain or shine.

ACCESS AND OPENING TIMES
The Harbour Bar is at 1-3 Sandside, Scarborough, YO11 1PE. It is open daily in summer until 6pm and every day except Weds in winter until 5pm (closed most of Nov and Dec).
theharbourbar.co.uk

HAT WORKS STOCKPORT

At one time, Stockport and its surrounding area was the centre of hatting excellence, fashioning titfers for young and old, work and play, sunshine and rain. Based in the old hatworks on Wellington Street, under a giant chimney saying 'HAT MUSEUM', Hat Works celebrates the industry that helped Stockport to get ahead.

The collection contains more than 400 hats and headpieces, from the humble flat cap to the most fashionable couture millinery. There are top hats, Stetsons, bathing caps, bicornes, tricornes, bonnets and bunnets, and a colourful display of international headgear.

There are tributes to famous – and infamous – hat wearers such as Chairman Mao, Tom Mix, Laurel and Hardy and Tony Hancock. Even better, there are famous hats such as Alexei Sayle's pork pie hat, Ainsley Harriott's chef's toque and Fred Dibnah's weatherbeaten flat cap.

There are also fascinating stories and memories from the factory's workers. Hatting was a difficult and dirty job – hot, dark, noisy and full of dangerous chemicals. 'Mad Hatters' were not just an invention of Lewis Carroll's, they were workers who developed dementia from the mercury used to prepare hatting felt. The process has a vocabulary all of its own, with

talk of blocking, pouncing, luring and trimming, hatter's bows and planking kettles.

The skills and artistry of the local industry is shown off in a hat block maker's workshop, moved lock, stock and barrel from William Plant and Co of Manchester – the last hat block makers in the North of England when they closed in 1976. Amidst the machines and lathes, the office is there too and vintage hat boxes sit in a beautifully preserved old-fashioned shop. It's an elegant way to top off a wonderfully rounded celebration of hats, hatters and hatting.

ACCESS AND OPENING TIMES
Hat Works is at Wellington Mill, Wellington St, Stockport, SK3 0EU. It is open Tues-Sat 10am-5pm, Sun 11am-5pm (closed Mondays, except bank holidays). stockport.gov.uk/hatworks

HOLY ISLAND NORTHUMBERLAND

A trip to the Holy Island of Lindisfarne is a real adventure. Linked to the mainland by a causeway, it is cut off every time the tide comes in. Racing the sea as you cross the alien landscape of sand and mudflats is an unexpectedly exotic experience, rewarded by what feels like a trip to another world.

To enjoy the island, leave your vehicle and your cares at the car park and start wandering. There are a few paths to take, depending on how long you want to walk and what you want to see. For a small island, there are so many stories here. Monks called it home, preaching Christianity from the priory. Now pilgrims follow in their footsteps, making

the challenging walk from the mainland barefoot across the sands. Lobster creels sit on the harbour wall, while upturned herring busses, an unofficial symbol of the island, serve as fishermen's sheds.

The castle dominates the skyline – a 16th-century fort sitting on a rocky pimple of land, surrounded by sea and farmland. It has long been a favourite of artists like Charles Rennie Mackintosh who came to paint the views, and Roman Polanski who set his film *Cul-de-Sac* here. Redeveloped in 1901 by Sir Edwin Lutyens for Edward Hudson, the founder of *Country Life* magazine, its Arts and Crafts decoration and Gertrude Jekyll-designed garden make it stand out.

Further on, beside the disused lime kilns, the beach is covered in teetering piles of stones as visitors make their own rocky pinnacle. From here you can walk back the way you came or go further into the heart of the island through farmland and wildlife-rich sand dunes.

The birds are cheeky here – wherever you go there's a rustling in the hedgerows and loud calls from skylarks, oystercatchers and chaffinches amongst others. The whole area is a National Nature Reserve, and two newly-built hides frame the wonderful views, providing shelter from the harsh winds.

As long as you get your timing right, a trip to Lindisfarne is a great way to get away from it all without having to travel too far. There is nowhere else quite like it.

ACCESS AND OPENING TIMES

Holy Island is east of the A1 between Berwick-upon-Tweed and Bamburgh. Access via the causeway is only possible at safe tide times. lindisfarne.org.uk

HORNSEA MUSEUM HORNSEA

In an old cottage on the main street, Hornsea Museum brightly tells the story of a small seaside town that became a big name in the world of ceramics. Among the period displays of life in old Hornsea sits the Hornsea Pottery Collection – the largest public collection of Hornsea Pottery in the world. The pottery was the town's biggest success story – a small but thriving family firm whose stylish yet affordable wares are now considered design classics.

In one of the museum's outbuildings are more than 2000 pieces, ranging from vases to eggcups, slipware to spice jars. The collection spans 50 years, and includes both highly collectable rare pieces and World's Best Plumber mugs.

The company was founded in 1949 when brothers Desmond and Colin Rawson started to make plaster of Paris seaside souvenirs. A year later, their friend Philip Clappison invested in it and, after a few years, brought in his son John, a bright ceramics student at Hull School of Art. He created their beautiful Elegance range while still in his teens, turning fashionable heads towards Hornsea. Soon newlyweds were opening Hornsea-produced crockery sets up and down the land.

Being a small operation, the pottery lacked the resources for hand-painting or transfer-printing, so John Clappison pioneered new shapes and techniques to make innovative, fashionable designs.

His experimentation with glazing led to the distinctive look of their bestselling Heirloom, Saffron and Bronte ranges, which came to epitomise the 1970s as much as *The Good Life* or Spangles. At one point, the Heirloom designs were so in demand that they had to be rationed.

After decades of success, the cracks began to show in the 1980s when a series of unfortunate business deals coincided with the rise of competition from Argos and other cheaper retailers. The company finally closed in 2000, but its legacy lives on. The ceramics (particularly Clappison's designs) are increasingly collectable, and Hornsea Pottery continues to be used in homes all over the world. The ceramics on display here are an absolute delight, and the story behind the big company from a little town makes for fascinating reading.

ACCESS AND OPENING TIMES

Hornsea Museum is at Burns Farm, 11-17 Newbegin, Hornsea, HU18 1AB. It is open Easter to October, weekdays 11am-5pm, Sat 10am-4pm and Sun 1pm-4pm. hornseamuseum.com

INGROW MUSEUM OF RAIL TRAVEL

KEIGHLEY

The Ingrow Museum of Rail Travel shows how rail travel has changed for ordinary people over the last hundred years. Through its careful preservation of historic railway carriages and the assiduous gathering of everyday bits and pieces of rail travel, it paints an evocative picture of life on the railways through the decades.

The focus on the passenger gives the museum a warm, personal feel. Visitors can backtrack through time in one of the nine beautifully-restored vintage carriages and imagine what it must have been like to be Victorian nobility off for some sea air or a 1940's evacuee heading to a quiet life in the country. Through clever displays and audio-visual presentations, the carriages come alive with stories – it's time travel through rail travel.

While the carriages might seem uncomfortable by today's standards, this was a step up from a horse and cart or Shanks's pony. As the railways

developed, so amenities such as toilets, electric lights and heating were added – luxury! On the platforms, smartly dressed dummies sit patiently beside piles of suitcases and hatboxes with only stewed tea and curly sandwiches for comfort, as classic posters advertise the age of the train.

The museum's roots go back to 1965, when a group of enthusiasts gathered together to save the rolling stock that was quickly disappearing from Britain's railways. They formed the Vintage Carriages Trust, which runs the museum today. The carriages are so carefully conserved and the railwayana so comprehensive that they are regularly used for filming period films and TV dramas.

The museum is beside Ingrow Station, the first stop after Keighley on the beautiful Keighley and Worth Valley Railway line, used in the 1970's film *The Railway Children*. A visit to the museum and the neighbouring Ingrow Loco Museum comes free with a Green Rover Ticket on the railway, so pack your picnic and make a day of it.

ACCESS AND OPENING TIMES

The Museum of Rail Travel is at Ingrow Railway Centre (on the main A629 between Keighley and Halifax), South Street, Keighley West Yorkshire, BD21 5AX. The shop and museum are open daily from 11am; last admission 4pm. vintagecarriagestrust.org

BUILT AT
SALTLEY
WORKS
1936
WAGON Cº Lº BIRMINGHAM

BR(E)
BUILDERS
STRATFORD
1950

BUILT IN 1912
BY G N Cº
0 TONS
70
BR-E

ROBERTS
Cº LTD 35
BUILDERS
SHEFIELD

8762

YORKSHIRE ENGINE Cº LIMITED
Nº 855
MEADOW HALL WORKS
1961
SHEFFIELD

NUMBER TAKERS

46249

RESTRICT
0

EAT CENTRAL

BEWARE

OF THE

TRAINS

20a 61

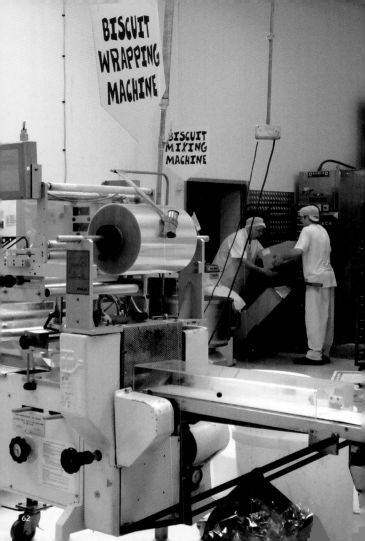

JOHN BULL BRIDLINGTON

John Bull Confectioners have been keeping the people of Bridlington sweet since 1911, when Ernest Hodgson opened a shop on Prince Street.

Named after the famous symbol of England, its wares were typical British seaside fare – humbugs, bonbons and flavoured rock. Ernest liked to show how his confections were made and was happy to explain one of life's sweetest mysteries – the secret of how letters get inside a stick of seaside rock.

More than 100 years later, the business is still going strong with 18 shops from Whitby to Weymouth. It's still in the family too, with Ernest's grandson Trevor overseeing operations like Yorkshire's own Willy Wonka. The business is too big for a back shop now, so there's a purpose-built viewing area inside John Bull's modern factory where visitors can still feast their eyes on this amazing spectacle.

At the viewing gallery, lots of excited faces (young and old) watch as the expert sweetmakers pour and pull great blobs of brightly coloured sugar into shape. Lettered rock is always handmade but man and machine work in harmony, as workers snip the mixture with huge sugar shears, drop it into a hypnotic pulling machine and then into what looks like a giant cigar-rolling contraption that pumps out long cables of molten rock to be gently rolled by hand into smooth sticks. Even after

seeing it, it seems like a modern miracle that something so malleable can turn into something so perfectly detailed and regular. For a small charge you make your own lettered rock – it's harder than it looks!

If that isn't enough sugary fun, you can also see biscuits and fudge being made, learn about the history of the company and take part in a retro sweets quiz which is bound to take everyone back to childhood if they're not there already. The staff hand out sweets and biscuits as Trevor looks on in his white trilby with the benevolent air of a man who gets to run a sweet factory for a living. At the end of all this, you can pick and mix some gifts from the well-stocked sweet shop and take away a taste of British seaside tradition.

ACCESS AND OPENING TIMES
John Bull Confectioners Ltd is at Unit 1, Lancaster Road, Carnaby Industrial Estate, Bridlington, YO15 3QY. It is generally open Easter to October weekdays 1pm-3pm during term-time, with an additional 11am-12pm session during school summer holidays. john-bull.com

KIELDER OBSERVATORY KIELDER

Kielder Observatory sits unobtrusively on top of a hill in Europe's largest man-made forest, far, far away from the traffic and streetlights that dim the urban night skies. Its main purpose is as a public observatory for experienced astronomers and enthusiastic novices to gaze skywards and search for a star.

Gary Fildes, the director of the observatory and Northumberland's answer to Professor Brian Cox, was drawn to Kielder Forest by its dark skies many moons ago. Nightwatch events at Kielder Castle were so enthusiastically received that he looked into the possibility of building an observatory here. With support from Peter Sharpe of Kielder Art

and Architecture, the idea became reality after an architectural competition was held to design a suitable building.

The competition was won by Charles Barclay Architects, who designed a sleek timber-clad building, solar- and wind-powered, and designed to fit into its sylvan surroundings. Somewhat Tardis-like inside, it contains two observatories and a presentation area. Viewing platforms outside look out over Kielder Water and onwards to the open skies.

There are two rotating telescopes – the Newtonian telescope is only one of three in the world. Dedicated to Sir Patrick Moore, the observatory opened in 2008 and won a Civic Trust Award for architecture shortly afterwards.

It now hosts regular sell-out events on aurora watching, solar astronomy and family star spotting. The events are run by Kielder Observatory Astronomical Society volunteers who travel from miles to share their interplanetary passion. The observatory was recently awarded coveted Dark Skies status, making it one of the best sites in England to go star spotting.

To get there, follow the road signs and continue up the winding path. Stop at James Turrell's Skyspace, an art installation intended to promote enjoyment of the sky above, whatever the weather. Sit back on the angled bench and watch the world go by. Remember that the observatory is remote and high up, so bring extra layers and come prepared for the darkness.

ACCESS AND OPENING TIMES

The observatory is on Black Fell, off Shilling Pot, Kielder, Northumberland, NE48 1EJ. It is open for pre-booked events; closed during daylight hours, though it is possible to park by Skyspace and walk up for the wide open views. kielderobservatory.org

THE LAUREL AND HARDY MUSEUM ULVERSTON

The former stage of the Roxy Cinema is the perfect location for a museum devoted to Stan Laurel, Ulverston's most famous son. It follows his life from birth as Arthur Stanley Jefferson in 1890 through adolescence treading the boards in British music halls to his world-famous cinema career in Hollywood.

Although the museum is in Stan's birthplace, it would be nothing without his screen partner Oliver Hardy (who has his own museum in Harlem, Georgia). They worked together on 107 films from 1921 to 1951, making a winning partnership on and off screen.

The museum has all the ramshackle charm of a Laurel and Hardy movie. It began as the collection of Ulverston's

mayor Bill Cubin, a lifelong Laurel and Hardy fan. He checked the local records and uncovered Stan's birthplace as Ulverston, not North Shields as previously thought. By 1983, Bill's collection was big enough to open to the public, and the Laurel and Hardy Museum was born.

Now owned by Bill's daughter Marion and run by her son Mark, it has grown over the years with great support from Laurel and Hardy fans the world over, including the fez-wearing Sons of the Desert, the international Laurel and Hardy appreciation society, who regularly make pilgrimages to Stan's birthplace. There are collectors' items and memorabilia, fan letters, and props

and photos from his personal life and film career. It is packed with interesting snippets and memories.

Perhaps most importantly, the films that made the duo famous play on repeat and red velvet cinema seats are provided for your viewing pleasure. The museum fills with chuckles as the hapless pair try to get that piano up those stairs again. Even though you know what's coming, it's funny every time. The perfectly-timed slapstick and cracking comedy lines that made them global stars are always top of the bill here, and Laurel and Hardy keep new visitors and old fans laughing, whether they are nine or ninety.

ACCESS AND OPENING TIMES

The Laurel & Hardy Museum is at On the Stage at the Roxy, Brogden St, Ulverston, LA12 7AH. Ulverston is on the A590 to Barrow-in-Furness. Standard opening hours are daily 10am-5pm (closed Mondays and Wednesdays). laurel-and-hardy.co.uk

LEVENS HALL CUMBRIA

Levens Hall in Cumbria is a country house with a difference. Beside the grand manor house are beautiful grounds where mature trees and well-maintained shrubs surround the world's oldest and finest topiary garden.

Topiary, the art of clipping shrubs and hedges into recognisable shapes, dates back to Roman times and reached its peak in the 17th and 18th centuries. The gardens at Levens Hall were designed in 1694 by Monsieur Guillaume Beaumont, a renowned gardener who laid out the gardens at Hampton Court and was head gardener for King James II. Levens is the only one of his gardens to survive. Many beautiful topiary gardens were replanted in the 18th century after a more natural, easier to maintain landscaped style came into fashion.

Today, visiting the topiary garden is like walking into a surreal kingdom. Yew and box hedges are clipped into more than 100 different shapes – geometric, animal and unidentifiable.

There are defined shapes such as pyramids and spirals, and creatures like birds and animals, but the most

intriguing residents are the wonderful amorphous blobs and surreal statues that pepper the garden like peculiar guardians waiting to spring into life.

Part of the joy of visiting is pondering what they are. It's like trying to see shapes in the clouds. Look out for the Great Umbrellas, the Judge's Wig and Queen Elizabeth and her Maids of Honour. Their close arrangement makes extended wanders along the paths rewarding, as there is something new to see from every angle.

Keeping the garden in shape is a full-time job for four gardeners. Trimming the hedges takes six months every year and involves scaffolding, 30-inch hedge trimmers and a great deal of care. There is also a rose garden, a nuttery, willow labyrinth and play area as well as the earliest recorded Ha-Ha (a sunken wall and ditch designed to create a barrier while preserving views). Traction engines are in steam every Sunday and Bank Holiday in the grounds. In the nearby park are herds of black fallow deer and feral rare-breed Bagot goats.

ACCESS AND OPENING TIMES

Levens Hall is near Kendal, Cumbria, LA8 0PD. The gardens are open April to October, Sun-Thurs 10am-5pm. levenshall.co.uk

THE LIT & PHIL

NEWCASTLE UPON TYNE

Newcastle's stately Lit and Phil is the largest independent library outside London. Founded in 1793 as the Literary and Philosophical Society of Newcastle upon Tyne it began as a conversation club for the intelligentsia of North East England.

The current building on Westgate Road opened in 1825 as meeting rooms with a library attached. It became an intellectual greenhouse for forward thinkers of the day such as Lord Armstrong, engineer and owner of the magnificent Cragside country house, and Sir Joseph Swan, whose invention of the incandescent lightbulb made the lecture theatre the first room to be lit by electric light in 1880. Oscar Wilde and John Betjeman were among the worthies to give talks here, and recent members include Pet Shop Boy, Neil Tennant, one of the brightest people in pop.

Libraries can be austere, forbidding places, but not the Lit and Phil. It is as welcoming as a favourite pub on a Sunday afternoon. The beautiful high-ceilinged reading rooms with their ornate roof lights immediately lift the spirits and open the mind. The aroma of coffee mingles with that of wood polish and leather – one breath makes you feel instantly smarter. Busts of former

members guard the stacks, almost nodding in approval.

The library now holds more than 150,000 books piled from floor to ceiling – everything from Icelandic Sagas to the latest crime fiction. Before you know it, you're running your fingers down an unfamiliar spine and picking up a new subject. Conversation is still encouraged too. Between the book stacks, members discuss everything from great works of literature to who's going to win the football, while others play games of chess or simply read quietly.

You might think that libraries have had their day, but the Lit and Phil's membership is the highest since 1952. New patron Alexander Armstrong, whose ancestors include two former presidents of the society, has recently led an appeal for funds. Donations are vital to maintain the beautiful listed building and continue the organisation's educational purpose. It has flexible membership schemes and a regular lecture series with talks on everything from creative writing to nasology (the study of noses). It is very welcoming to impromptu visitors, so pop in next time you're in Newcastle to enjoy its special brand of quiet.

ACCESS AND OPENING TIMES

The Lit & Phil is at 23 Westgate Road, Newcastle, NE1 1SE and is open Mon-Sat from 9.30am – closing times vary. litandphil.org.uk/index.shtml

MARKS IN TIME LEEDS

The Michael Marks Building at the
University of Leeds houses a company
archive. But this isn't any company
archive, this is the Marks & Spencer
company archive, which tells the story of
how one of Britain's favourite retailers
grew from a Leeds market stall into a
multi-million-pound global corporation.

Through a series of displays, as
carefully designed as one of their stores,
the exhibition tells the story of M&S
from the moment Michael Marks
opened his first Penny Bazaar in Leeds
Kirkgate Market in 1884. His eye for sales
and merchandising, coupled with Tom
Spencer's business sense, created a
winning partnership which became a
worldwide success story.

The exhibition shows how M&S has
grown and diversified through two
World Wars and various economic ups
and downs to keep its position as one of
Britain's best-loved retailers.

There are amazing vintage products on
show and fascinating facts about the

New Look Dress
This 'New Look' dress shows the optimism of postwar Britain. Unlike utility clothing, it uses a lot of
fabric and features tucks and folds that would never
have been allowed during rationing.

company, told from the eyes of staff and shoppers. The people behind the brand all have their story to tell – from the researchers who conducted the National Leg Survey to help tights fit better to the scientists who developed the perfect chocolate fondant and the designers who packaged it up.

The secrets of M&S's enduring success are hinted at – treat staff well, adapt to the times and invest in research and development. All in all, it is much more than just a company archive. It's a story of social history, product development, design, fashion and business, related through revolutionary changes in ordinary lives – machine washable fabrics, frozen chickens, the liberating introduction of slacks and the sweet moment that Percy Pigs first hit the shelves. This fantastic collection shows why Marks & Spencer has rightly become part of the fabric of British life.

ACCESS AND OPENING TIMES

Marks & Spencer Company Archive is in the Michael Marks Building, University of Leeds, LS2 9JT (sat nav LS2 9LZ). The archive is open Mon-Fri 10am-5pm and on Saturdays for special events. marksintime.marksandspencer.com

Please do not touch

MARSDEN GROTTO SOUTH SHIELDS

Billed as Europe's only fine dining restaurant in a cave, Marsden Grotto in South Shields certainly is unique.

Built into the rock at the foot of a cliff, the grotto has served as a hostelry for smugglers and more salubrious visitors for more than 200 years. Walk down the 137 zigzag steps or take the lift if you prefer, and enjoy a drink in this shady nook.

Looking out onto Marsden Bay and Marsden Rock, the calm cliffs above belie the fact that this little corner is all action. The waves come crashing onto the pebbly beach, while the nesting seabirds caw relentlessly. It's not a quiet spot exactly, but it's got an unexpected drama about it, like finding a secret shelter with an exclusive view.

Inside, the grotto is on two floors. On the ground floor the Cave Bar is hewn out of the rock and covered with nautical paraphernalia. It's so atmospheric you half expect to see Captain Jack Sparrow supping some rum with Fred Flintstone. Upstairs is a more polished restaurant which is available for hire.

The history of the grotto goes back to 1782 when local troglodyte Jack the Blaster turned a small cave into a family home using explosives from a nearby mine. The story goes that he also liked to sell drinks to passing smugglers who could hide their contraband in the cave, and the grotto's boozy history began.

In 1826, a man called Peter Allen turned the modest dwelling into a 15-room mansion and opened it properly as an inn. Later still, Sunderland brewery Vaux took over, improving the standard of the building in the 1930s and adding the lift that still runs today. Since then it has changed hands numerous times, before opening as it is today in 2008 as a pub and seafood restaurant. Legend has it that the ghosts of smugglers live on to this day, so watch out for a different kind of spirit being served at the bar.

ACCESS AND OPENING TIMES

Marsden Grotto is on the Coast Road, South Shields, NE34 7BS and is open daily for lunch 12pm-3pm and for dinner 6pm-11pm.

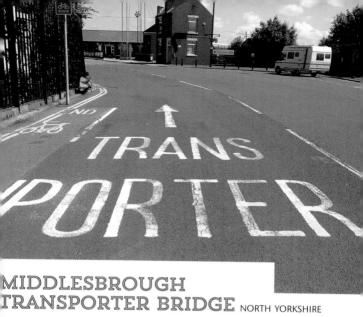

MIDDLESBROUGH
TRANSPORTER BRIDGE NORTH YORKSHIRE

Bridges never quite get the acclaim they deserve, considering how beautiful they are and what a wonderful job they do. None more so than the Middlesbrough Transporter Bridge (also known as the Tees Transporter Bridge) – vital transport link, spectacular piece of engineering and local icon.

Visible for miles around, the bridge is a much-loved symbol of Middlesbrough, pictured on the town's badge above the slogan 'Moving forward' – an enduring reminder of its industrial heart, pulsing back and forth across the Tees connecting Middlesbrough on the south bank to Port Clarence on the north.

Built by Sir William Arrol and Company, who also designed the Forth Bridge and Tower Bridge, it opened in 1911. There were only 20 transporter bridges in the world and all were constructed between 1893 and 1916. Their design allowed vehicles and passengers to cross a river without obstructing access for boats. Middlesbrough's is one of three in Britain (the others are in Newport and Warrington) and the longest of only eight left worldwide.

Between four sturdy blue legs, a small gondola carries 200 people, nine cars, or six cars and one minibus, across 259.3m,

teetering 48.7m above the Tees. Running roughly every 15 minutes, it takes two minutes or so to reach the other side. For a great, galumphing thing it moves very gracefully, and the journey is refreshingly relaxed. Passengers and cars share the same deck and you're free to mill around enjoying the view as the gondola whirrs its way across the river.

For years it was rather taken for granted, but in 1985 it was Grade II listed and in 1993 was awarded the Institution of Mechanical Engineers' highest honour, The Heritage Plaque, for engineering excellence. It has also been celebrated in popular culture, most famously in the North East TV drama *Auf Wiedersehen Pet*, where a storyline about the bridge being dismantled and moved

to Arizona created some degree of alarm

Even, if you don't need to cross, it's still worth visiting. An information centre explains the history of the bridge and the Winding House shows off the cables that power it – such a simple mechanism, but so graceful and powerful. On special days the walkway at the top is open to walk across or for brave souls keen to bungee-jump or abseil from its heights.

ACCESS AND OPENING TIMES
The Tees Transporter Bridge is on Ferry Road, Middlesbrough, TS2 1PL. It is worth checking travel information before visiting, as it is sometimes closed in bad weather or for maintenance. middlesbrough.gov.uk/transporterbridge

MIDLAND HOTEL MORECAMBE

The Midland Hotel is Morecambe's jewel in the crown. Built beside what was the rail terminus (now the Platform entertainment venue) by the London, Midland and Scottish Railway company, it was designed to attract style-conscious travellers to the North West's riviera for sunshine and sea views.

Architect Oliver Hill was inspired by the modern architecture he saw on a trip to Sweden. Combining the clean lines of the new Streamline Moderne style with contemporary building techniques, it was designed to turn heads. The Midland sits proudly on the prom, all graceful curves and white stucco. When it opened in

1933, it caused quite a stir. The local paper proclaimed that it was 'Morecambe's Great White Hope' and *Architecture Illustrated* magazine devoted 33 pages to it.

The lack of decoration outside (barring the two elegant seahorses above the entrance) is made up for inside, where nautical themed décor by fashionable artists of the 1930s make the Midland a cut above your usual high-class hotel. Panels and reliefs by Eric Gill decorate the lobby, along with seahorse mosaics and wave-themed rugs by Marion Dorn. The simplicity and bright colours of the designs bring lightness and an instant

sense of joy, while the nautical themes combine with the open views for an unmistakable breath of fresh air.

There are more beautiful touches throughout the building. A quirky map of the North West by Eric Gill adorns the function suite and a lost mural by Eric Ravilious has been repainted in the bar.

During its heyday, socialites and stars such as Noel Coward and Coco Chanel would travel miles to visit. For years it was the place to be – until changing tastes and accessible foreign holidays saw its fortunes decline. After the war and a brief spell as a military hospital, each change of ownership steered the Midland in a new direction. The choppy waters of British tourism were hard to navigate and in the 1990s it finally closed.

Its future looked bleak for a while

and the building lay derelict until architectural renewal company Urban Splash stepped in. They carefully repaired the original features and added modern touches to create a building that feels as contemporary as it did when it opened, without being an Art Deco time capsule. The prime position and unique design ensure that there are fine views inside and out. Since reopening in 2008, it has led Morecambe's regeneration and once again crowns its promenade. Now managed by English Lakes Hotels, it is a great place to stay. The bar and restaurant are open to non-residents.

ACCESS AND OPENING TIMES
The Midland is on Marine Road West, Morecambe LA4 4BU.
englishlakes.co.uk/hotels/lancashire-hotels/the-midland-hotel-morecambe/

NATIONAL GLASS CENTRE SUNDERLAND

National Glass Centre at the University of Sunderland celebrates one of the North East's great unsung industries. An abundance of cheap coal and lime, as well as easy access for imports and exports through the port, meant that the glass industry was a major local employer until the last factory closed in 2007.

The decline in the industry prompted fears that local expertise would be lost, so the Arts Council-funded centre opened in 1998 with the aim of becoming the national centre of glass-making excellence. Former workers from Wearside's factories mingle with artists and students from the University of Sunderland's Glass and Ceramics Department, which is based here, to ensure that years of knowledge are passed onto a new generation and can grow with state-of-the-art equipment and support.

The centre traces the history of glass-making from 674AD when Sunderland's patron saint, Benedict Biscop, commissioned decorative windows for St Peter's Church, through to the production of bottles, plate glass, souvenir glass and decorative collectable pieces.

One notable local success was Pyrex, a special heat-resistant glass made here by Jobling & Co under licence from Corning in the USA. This tough but fashionable material was a winner in kitchens

worldwide, and it is refreshing to see casserole dishes on display alongside more rarefied glass products. There are all kinds of glass on display here – old and new, crude and delicate, mass-produced and handmade, domestic and scientific.

Free glass-making demonstrations show exactly how delicate and complex glasswork can be. The heat is incredible and the artistry is amazing. It takes years of learning to handle such a fragile substance with such apparent ease – it's hot, dirty work to turn a blob of molten glass into a covetable artwork.

Leading glass and ceramic artists also have studio space here and changing

exhibitions showcase their work, along with celebrations of glass in all different shapes and sizes, from snowglobes to spectacles.

It's a fascinating mix. A glass roof tops the building off nicely, making National Glass Centre a clear winner.

ACCESS AND OPENING TIMES
National Glass Centre is on Liberty Way, Sunderland, SR6 0GL. It is open daily 10am-5pm and admission is free.
nationalglasscentre.com

The Dan Klein and Alan J. Poole Collection

PEASHOLM PARK SCARBOROUGH

Peasholm Park is one of the loveliest public parks to be found anywhere in Britain. Most of the time, it is the very epitome of calm. At its centre, a hilltop pagoda looks out over a circular lake, while a statue of Buddha keeps watch outside the café.

On the lake there be dragons – but they are peaceful ones in the shape of boats that you can pedal round the island, with dragon lamps to light the way. It's an unexpected taste of the Orient in North Yorkshire.

Opened in 1912, the park's Japanese theme is said to be based on the blue and white Willow Pattern plate which was popular at the time. Harry W Smith, the borough engineer, planned the park in 1911 and Japanese statues and shrubs were brought in to add an exotic flavour. The pagoda followed in 1929 and lasted for 70 years before it was burned down in 1999, the same year that the park was Grade II listed. Heritage Lottery funding and a great deal of care and attention has recently brought the park back to its former glory.

On special occasions, the lake is home to the Peasholm Park Naval Warfare, taking place since 1927. Charismatic compère David Hale sets the scene from

a floating platform, playing a selection of popular hits on an electronic organ. As the fleet, billing itself as 'the world's smallest manned Navy', enters the water, he whips the audience up into a panto-style frenzy so that they are ready to cheer the allies and boo the unspecified 'baddies' as the battle begins.

Over the next half hour, 6m-long replica boats, steered by council employees, recreate the Battle of the River Plate, with special appearances by the RAF, real explosions and a supporting cast of civilian ducks and geese. It is proper theatre, and something for all ages to enjoy.

Beyond the lake, there are pretty landscaped gardens with a wilder walk through the glen, full of mature trees, chirruping birds and overconfident squirrels. It is a particularly pleasing combination of attractions – generous public spaces for the party animals, putting and boating if you're feeling sporty, secluded walks for the quiet types and ample opportunities for ice cream and cold drinks. It's the kind of park that works all year round, in every weather.

ACCESS AND OPENING TIMES
Peasholm Park is at North Bay, Scarborough, YO12 7TR; the main entrance is on Peasholm Drive. It is open all day every day.
peasholmpark.com

PIEL ISLAND FURNESS

Piel Island sits at the tip of the Furness Peninsula, half a mile from the mainland, a few miles from Barrow-in-Furness and light years away from the rest of the world. There is a row of pilots cottages, a pub and a castle with nothing else between apart from flocks of wading birds feasting on the rich sands of Morecambe Bay.

Daytrippers arrive by ferry from Roa Island (on the mainland) in high season, or on foot from Walney Island all year round (the latter only possible with care at low tide).

The island is steeped in history which is half-erased by the sands of time. Only the most stubborn traces are visible, such as the ruins of the impressive 14th-century castle and the sturdy Ship Inn, where the landlord and landlady are crowned the King and Queen of Piel.

This odd regal tradition dates back to a visit by Lambert Simnel, a pretender to the English throne who stopped here in 1487 on the way from Ireland. The King and Queen of Piel are crowned unceremoniously with a pint of beer over their heads. Their throne sits in the pub beside a majestic cabinet of curiosities showing off the island's

CAST OFF

LOST & FOUND

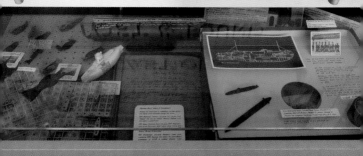

PROLIFERATION

crown jewels – stuffed seabirds, shipbuilding paraphernalia from nearby Barrow-in-Furness and other found treasures that have been washed ashore.

The island was owned by the Duke of Buccleuch until 1919, when it was gifted to the town of Barrow-in-Furness as a memorial to those who lost their lives in the First World War.

ACCESS AND OPENING TIMES
To get there, you can catch the 12-seater ferry which zips across the Piel Channel from Roa Island in high season or walk across the muddy causeway from Walney Island at low tide (take care as the tide comes in at quite a lick). pielisland.co.uk

THE POISON GARDEN ALNWICK

If you think of gardens as places to relax and commune with nature, The Alnwick Garden's Poison Garden might make you change your mind. Inside locked gates marked 'These plants can kill', the garden looks innocent enough, but has a deadly secret. Because of this, it is only accessible by guided tour lest its contents cause a fatality.

The poisonous properties of some plants are well known – hemlock and deadly nightshade are known no-nos. However, others are so commonplace that their lethal properties are rather alarming. Did you know that rhubarb leaves can kill you instantly or that Laurel bushes give off deadly cyanide gas when burnt? The guides' tales of floral fatalities are so surprising they're almost funny until you realise they're true.

The Poison Garden also contains plants that irritate, such as nettles and lilies, or that intoxicate, such as juniper berries and wormwood, used to flavour gin and absinthe.

Some poisonous plants can be helpful when used wisely – one seed from the Ricinus communis plant is enough to kill

THESE PLANTS CAN KILL

you, but used properly it makes castor oil. Salicin from the bark of the willow tree becomes aspirin, invaluable in small quantities, deadly if overdosed. Some plants are considered so dangerous that growing them is illegal. The cannabis sativa plant can only be grown here under licence from the Home Office.

The Duchess of Northumberland, who owns the estate, created the garden as a twist on the traditional apothecary's garden. She wanted to complement the growing understanding of healing plants with knowledge of nature's darker side – a horrible history of poisonous plants being of special interest to children who enjoy a gruesome tale.

The garden was designed by Jacques and Peter Wirtz, with plants by garden historian Caroline Holmes. It opened in 2005 as part of the wider development of The Alnwick Garden, which is a joy to visit.

A tour of the Poison Garden is a truly
peculiar experience that entertains and
educates, and means you never look at
plants in quite the same way again.

ACCESS AND OPENING TIMES
The Alnwick Garden is on Denwick Lane,
Alnwick NE66 1YU. It is open
daily in spring/summer 10am-7pm
and in autumn/winter 12pm-6pm;
closed for much of January.
alnwickgarden.com

PONTEFRACT
LIQUORICE FESTIVAL PONTEFRACT

One day every year in July, Pontefract comes together to celebrate liquorice – the West Yorkshire town's black gold.

Market stalls in the town centre sell it in all shapes and sizes – allsorts, you could say. There are liquorice comfits, whips, cables, catherine wheels and those odd blue and pink liquorice allsorts that always gather at the bottom of the box. Pontefract or Pomfret Cakes, named after

the town and stamped with a picture of the castle, are sold in abundance.

You can also find liquorice fudge and liquorice chicken, and drink liquorice beer in the Liquorice Bush pub while stiltwalkers with hats shaped like liquorice allsorts patrol the town centre. If this gets too much, escape the crowds in Pontefract Museum, a beautiful Art Nouveau building which is full of

liquorice tins, as well as glassware and old artefacts unrelated to the town's famous export.

Originally introduced by monks as a medicinal herb, liquorice grew well in Pontefract's deep sandy soil and was turned into small discs. In 1760, when local chemist George Dunhill mixed liquorice with sugar to make a sort of medicinal sweet, Pomfret Cakes went into commercial production and a new industry was born.

Dunhills quickly became one of the biggest producers of liquorice sweets, with Pontefract Cakes hand-stamped until the mid-20th century. Soon there were 13 factories in the town and the phenomenon was even immortalised in Sir John Betjeman's poem 'The Liquorice Fields of Pontefract'. For the next few decades the factories turned out all

shapes and sizes of liquorice until production declined in the 1960s.

Today there are only two factories left – Haribo, formerly Dunhills, and Tangerine, formerly Monkhills, now part of Cadbury Trebor Bassett. Both are linked by a street called Liquorice Way. Liquorice has not been grown locally since the early 1970s and is now imported from Europe, but there are rumours that it is to be grown locally once more. Whether this happens or not, it is never far away and a trip to the Liquorice Festival is a chance to taste Pontefract's sweet history for yourself.

ACCESS AND OPENING TIMES
Pontefract is in the metropolitan borough of Wakefield, near both the M62 and the A1. yorkshire.com/places/wakefield/pontefract

PORT SUNLIGHT THE WIRRAL

Port Sunlight is a model village on the Wirral. It is a little bubble of idealism, a social and architectural wonder, and a very pleasant place to visit.

It was created when Lever Brothers (now Unilever) began looking for factory premises to cope with the popularity of their new product,

Sunlight Soap. When they found some marshy ground on the Wirral, close to a river and a railway line, they knew it wa the perfect spot.

William Hesketh Lever, the driving force behind the company, wanted a community for his workers to socialise and improve themselves in a wholesome

Christian way. He saw investing his profits
in good-quality workers' housing as
'prosperity sharing' – a chance to improve
lives through ideal homes, pleasant
surroundings and opportunities for
education and recreation.

Inaugurated in 1888, and constructed
between 1899 and 1914, more than 800
self-contained houses were built, along
with a new factory and various public
buildings for 3500 workers. A keen art
collector, Lever's interest in the Arts and
Crafts Movement and his socialist ideals
influenced the style of the village. More
than 30 different architects were
employed to create blocks that go

together without being 'samey'. Each house, amazingly, is unique, but all share certain features like green space in front and a garden behind. Embellishments such as oriel windows, barley-sugar chimneys and ornamental plasterwork are just enough to make ordinary brick houses special without being gaudy. Even the factory looks good.

The whole effect is like a breath of fresh air. It is so green and clean and peaceful that the streets beyond, with their sirens and neon signs, suddenly feel like another world. It's like seeing a model village full size. The backs of the houses aren't visible from the road so every street puts its best face forward. There are no garden fences, and front doors are often very close together, promoting neighbourliness. There are open spaces and trees everywhere, and

uplifting public art in the central avenue.

Port Sunlight was made a conservation area in 1978 and, even though most of the houses are owned privately now, the village retains its original character without feeling like it's stuck in the past. The Port Sunlight Museum (formerly the Girls' Club) tells the story of this fascinating place and the magnificent Lady Lever Art Gallery collects some of the art that influenced its style. A wander round the village's beautiful streets is a fascinating glimpse at an ideal world.

ACCESS AND OPENING TIMES

Port Sunlight Museum is at 23 King George's Drive, Wirral, CH26 5DX, and is open daily 10am-5pm. The village is well signposted and has a railway station. portsunlightvillage.com

PRESTON BUS STATION PRESTON

Preston Bus Station is the largest bus station in Britain and definitely the most controversial. Opinions on its merit, or lack of it, range from architecture critics who love its uncompromising Brutalist form to angry passengers who loathe its foreboding walkways, bum-numbing

seats and useless stopped clocks.

Love it or hate it, you can't miss it. It i enormous. The concrete balconies stretch on for what seems like miles, sheltering stands for 80 buses. With fiv storeys, the upper floors have enough space for 1100 cars. Walking inside is lil

tering a cathedral. It's the oddest
eling to find somewhere at rush hour
at should be noisy and bustling but is
vernous and peaceful.
Built for a population explosion that
ver came, it has been dogged by
ntroversy ever since it opened in 1969.

Its use of *béton brut* – unpainted, raw
concrete – was a bold fashion statement,
but decades later many Brutalist
buildings have fallen out of favour,
unable to assuage the critics who see
them as hideous carbuncles too big to
hide and too costly to maintain. This

makes the survivors all the more precious to those who want to conserve them.

The amazing thing is that a building that seems so monstrous to some can inspire such a wealth of adoration in others. The Save Preston Bus Station group has supporters locally and internationally, and The Twentieth Century Society, architect Richard Rogers and the *Guardian* newspaper (which wrote a leader column in support of its listing) have all spoken out in its favour. Photographers and filmmakers flock to capture its curves and document its daily comings and goings. By 2012 it was on the World Monument Fund's list of sites at risk. Quite an achievement for a humble bus station.

After a particularly bleak period when it looked like the building was set for demolition, it was finally listed by English Heritage in September 2013. Its future is still uncertain, but it looks more hopeful with funding earmarked for its improvement and many supportive voices interested in securing its place in Preston's future.

ACCESS AND OPENING TIMES
Preston Bus Station is on Titheburn Street, Preston, PR1 1YT.
prestonbusstation.co.uk

THE RHUBARB TRIANGLE

At Oldroyds Farm in Carlton, Janet Oldroyd-Hulme leaves no rhubarb facts unearthed in her 90-minute farm tour. Its propagation, cultivation, suitability for freezing, recipe ideas and health properties are all covered in detail. Amuse your friends with rhubarb facts – yes it's true, it is actually a vegetable!

Oldroyds Farm sits proudly in the Rhubarb Triangle – an area of Yorkshire covering 14km between Wakefield, Rothwell and Morley. The triangle used to stretch between Leeds, Bradford and Wakefield and 90 percent of the world's forced rhubarb was cultivated here. Native to Siberia, it thrives in the cold wet Yorkshire climate and was fed by a rich supply of 'shoddy' wool from the local mills – a waste product made from recycled rags which was rich in nitrogen.

After the talk, it's time to visit the forcing sheds where the stems grow so quickly that you can sometimes hear them. The only light allowed in the sheds is a series of low candles, and the self-styled 'High Priestess of Rhubarb' continues her talk at a reverent whisper. The forced rhubarb grown here is a delicacy as it is more tender and its stalks are white in colour due to the lack of light.

It turns out the world of rhubarb is full of highs and lows. It was so sought after in the 1930s that special 'Rhubarb Express' trains ran fresh crops down to London overnight. However, a nation raised on rhubarb had its taste buds awakened by new, exciting tropical fruits introduced after the Second World War. Rhubarb languished on the shelves, and the number of growers crumbled.

Today, the Rhubarb Triangle is a scaled-down version of its former self, but it is enjoying a resurgence as more people decide to grow their own and restaurants turn to seasonally-produced local food.

In February 2010 Yorkshire Forced Rhubarb was awarded Protected Designation of Origin (PDO) status by the European Commission's Protected Food Name scheme, putting it in the same special class as Champagne and Parma Ham.

Oldroyd's tours run during the forced rhubarb season from January to March, and as part of the Wakefield Food Festival in February (booking is essential).

ACCESS AND OPENING TIMES

E. Oldroyd & Sons Ltd is close to the M62 at Ashfield Farm, Main Street, Carlton, WF3 3RW.

yorkshirerhubarb.co.uk

SALFORD LADS CLUB SALFORD

Salford Lads Club is a remarkable place in many ways. The oldest surviving boys' club in Britain, its motto 'To brighten young lives and make good citizens' has been quietly delivered by volunteers for more than 100 years.

Its famous doorway, immortalised on the gatefold cover of The Smiths' *The Queen is Dead* album leads into a surprisingly airy, perfectly preserved Edwardian interior – 'the most complete example of this rare form of social provision to survive in England', according to English Heritage. Corridors

go off in all directions with a football pitch, concert hall, dance studio, billiard room, boxing ring, and games rooms all nestled inside. Kids' voices ricochet round the high ceilings like the sound of a school at playtime. There are activities in every corner, with all visitors encouraged to try something they enjoy.

The club was founded by local philanthropists, the Groves Brothers, and opened in 1904 by Sir Robert Baden-Powell, who later went on to found the Scout movement. 'Lads clubs', as boys' clubs were known in

Manchester, were designed to keep lads who started work at 14 in those days) off the street and involved in healthy pursuits. Salford Girls assembled next door until their club was bombed in the blitz and never rebuilt.

In the Junior Games Room, Salford lads peer back from hundreds of photos, one for each year of summer camps. There are many famous sons – Graham Nash and Allan Clarke from the Hollies came here, as did actor Albert Finney and Peter Hook of New Order who lived a few doors down. However,

it was four Manchester lads that put the Club on the music map after Stephen Wright's picture of the Smiths slouched outside introduced the building to a new audience.

Today, Smiths fans from the world over make the pilgrimage to stand gloomily in front of its famous green doors or to visit the 'Smiths Room', specially created as an informal shrine for the Morrissey and Marr-minded. This was once the Weights Room, and is still home to barbells and snaps of greased-up bodybuilders such as Tony Holland, a

Salford lad who found fame as Mr Muscle on *Opportunity Knocks*.

Post-its, posters and photos from an altogether weedier crowd mingle with the musclemen, covering the room from floor to ceiling – a marriage that Morrissey would likely approve of. Whether you like the Smiths music or not, the devotion is a sight to behold. The way that these shy fans are welcomed into the club's delightfully informal interior mirrors the inclusive nature of the club itself. There's a place for everyone here.

ACCESS AND OPENING TIMES

Salford Lads' Club is on St Ignatius Walk Salford, Lancashire, M5 3RX. The club is open daily to members and also holds open days; to arrange a visit, contact the club (free but donations welcome). salfordladsclub.org.uk

TO BRIGHTEN YOUNG LIVES AND MAKE GOOD CITIZENS

Awards for Lifts

SALTBURN-BY-THE-SEA
CLIFF LIFT AND PIER

Saltburn-by-the-Sea is a coastal gem, as beautiful as the best southern seaside resorts, but not as well known. Slightly unexpected in this part of the industrial North East, its popularity exploded when the railway came here in 1861. The Victorian architecture is beautifully preserved and everything looks as fresh as it did 100 years ago.

To get to the beach and pier, travel in style on Saltburn's Cliff Lift, which transports visitors gracefully down the 36.5m drop in dainty cars with wooden seats and stained glass windows. The funicular railway is the oldest operating waterbalance cliff lift in Britain. Designed in 1884 by George Croydon Marks of the Richard Tangye Company, who installed many funiculars along the coast, it travels down a 71 percent incline, powered by the balance of water between the two cars and watched over by a brakeman in the cabin at the top.

At the bottom, the most northerly

...urviving pleasure pier in Britain has been ...veathering the storms since 1869. Now ...ess than half its original length, it ...tretches for 200m over a spotless sandy ...each – there are amusements at the ...ntrance, but apart from that it heads out ...o sea with little ornament. At least it did ...ntil the Saltburn Yarnbombers struck.

The unadorned railings were too much ...emptation for naughty knitters who ...elebrated the London 2012 Olympics ...y decorating them with a 50m-long ...carf of woollen figures, including ...nitted synchronised swimmers and a ...voolly Torvill and Dean. Since the first ...ruption of knitted wonderment, there ...ave been more – one for the Queen's ...iamond Jubilee, a summer holiday ...pecial with knitted fish and chips, ...each huts, and donkeys called Knit and ...url, and a World Cup preview in 2014.

These benevolent vandals bring a little touch of colour to an already special place. Passers-by stop to admire their handiwork, take a photo or give the figures a wee squeeze. The close-knit community is tight-lipped over the identity of the perpetrators, so who knows when they will strike next.

With the surf reportedly the best outside Cornwall, Saltburn is anything but stuffy, and a timeless mixture of generations happily mingles on the seafront. It is a coastal gem which is worth a visit at any time of the year.

ACCESS AND OPENING TIMES
Saltburn Cliff Lift is at Lower Prom, Saltburn, TS12 2QX. It is open daily in summer and at weekends in winter, 11am-5pm. saltburnbysea.com

THE SCARBOROUGH FAIR COLLECTION SCARBOROUGH

It's difficult to find words that make the Scarborough Fair Collection sound as brilliant as it actually is. The words 'steam museum' would put many visitors off, but persevere and don't be dissuaded by its anonymous location in a caravan park on the Scarborough-Filey road.

Inside the nondescript shed is a bright, shiny world of music and fun. A world-class collection of operational vintage fairground rides, steam engines and cinema organs is spread over three large rooms, complete with dancefloor. Organ music fills the air, immediately conjuring up all the fun of the fair.

The steam organs range from the hulking goliaths of the showmen's engines – 'Mighty in Strength and Endurance' according to the gaudy lettering on the Iron Maiden – to the delicately decorated dance organs. The rare European musical organs made by Decap, Mortier, Gavioli, Ruth and Marenghi are confections of curlicues and cherubs with a million tiny parts tinkling and tweeting away to make the sweetest sounds. The music sits at the back, like giant phonebooks of punched card – you would never think something that looked so ordinary could make such a beautiful sound.

Beside the dancefloor, the Art Deco stylings of the Decap Willem Tell organ

have come all the way from Antwerp. On a smaller scale, the awesome Action Man Orchestra is a sight to behold.

Pride of place goes to the Mighty Wurlitzers. The organist entertains for the Wednesday Tea Dance, as well as concerts throughout the year where the distinctive sound of the Wurlitzer

instantly transports you into another, more glamorous world.

The man behind the music is Graham Atkinson, a steam enthusiast who has travelled the world to gather his collection. His passions began when he used machines to entertain his holiday park customers. With other members of

e Fair Organ Preservation Society
notto: 'Whilst looking into the future,
us not forget the glories of the past'),
e future of these magnificent machines
n safe hands.

ACCESS AND OPENING TIMES
The Collection can be found at Flower
of May Holiday Park, Lebberston Cliff, on
the A165 between Scarborough and
Filey, North Yorkshire, YO11 3NU.
It is open March to November,
Wed-Sun 10am-4pm.
scarboroughfaircollection.com

SHIPLEY GLEN TRAMWAY SHIPLEY

This lovely little cable tramway is one of the oldest of its type in Britain, delighting visitors since 1895.

Located in the West Yorkshire town of Shipley, just north of Bradford, Shipley Glen was a different world back then. Pleasure-seekers would take the tram up the hill to find fantastic pleasure grounds, where thrill rides such as the Switchback Railway, Aerial Glide and Toboggan Slide, billed as the 'Longest, Widest and Steepest ever erected on Earth' awaited. For the more risk-averse, there were beautiful Japanese gardens and bracing walks on the spectacular rock formations. No wonder people flocked here from miles around.

The tramway was devised by showman Sam Wilson, who also managed the funfair. This feat of clever Victorian engineering transported as many as 17,000 visitors a day in the simple red and blue 'toastrack'-style ca that still run today. Competition from theme parks and exotic foreign holiday mean that the fair itself is long gone, but the tramway has clung on against the odds. When you realise how much has been lost here, its survival is nothin short of miraculous.

Following a long decline and closure in 1966 and 1986, its fortunes were up and down until the transport-loving enthusiasts of the Bradford Trolleybus Association pulled in to save the day. They steered the tramway to expansio

with new buildings in 1987 and a successful centenary in 1995. In 2002 the tramway was taken over by volunteers and a major rebuild in 2009-11 means that today passengers can enjoy Victorian transport running to 21st-century standards.

The full history of the tramway is on display in the station museum at the bottom, with a great mix of fun things for kids to play with and transportation facts to keep tramspotters amused.

Cars run on demand to the top where there's a chance to pick and mix traditional sweets from the shop before heading into Shipley Glen and Baildon Moor for a bracing walk.

If you're heading the other way, cross the majestic Roberts Park and the River Aire to beautiful Saltaire, a UNESCO World Heritage Site containing textile workers' houses and Salts Mill with its David Hockney Gallery.

Whether you are using the tramway a a shortcut for a woodland walk or admiring it as a feat of engineering it's ride back in time that really can't be matched anywhere else.

ACCESS AND OPENING TIMES

Shipley Glen's upper station is located off Prod Lane, Baildon, Shipley, BD17 5BN; the lower station can be accessed from Salts Grammar School car park. It open weekends 12pm-4.30pm and take special bookings at other times. shipleyglentramway.co.uk

SPURN NATIONAL NATURE RESERVE HUMBERSIDE

Spurn National Nature Reserve, or Spurn Head as it's also known, is a long strip of land curling out from the Holderness Coast into the Humber Estuary. The coastline is fragile around this part of East Yorkshire, nowhere more so than at Spurn. At 5km long and only 15m wide in places, it is so thin it is hardly there at all.

A veritable geography field trip in action, it is formed by the longshore drift that washes sediment down the east coast into the North Sea. It is always on the move, travelling west at the speed of 2m a year. Few things last here – whole towns have been washed away and whatever's left is living on borrowed time. Two disused lighthouses hang on stubbornly; wartime gun emplacements topple into the marram grass, and an old army railway runs erratically across what's left of the road – a sign of how far the land has moved in recent decades.

On the fat teardrop of land where the point finally disappears into the sea is one of Britain's only full-time lifeboat crews with the lifeboat kept 'at sea' to respond to emergencies. Pilot boats come and go from the jetty, beside the deliciously soft sandy beach. Wading birds and quiet walkers mingle as the roar of the wind and sea create a sort of natural white noise. The point is managed by the Yorkshire Wildlife Trust and is a special protection area – home to thousands of birds and other animals, with everything from wheatears to whales.

Philip Larkin, local miserablist and renowned poet, loved to come here, cycling all the way from his beloved Hull. The Larkin Trail, a series of plaques commemorating places close to his heart, ends here.

A visit to Spurn is a chance to get away from it all in a natural way, before turning back to the real world.

ACCESS AND OPENING TIMES

Spurn Head is south of Kilnsea, Hull, East Yorkshire, HU12 0UH. Following the 2013 tidal surge, the road to Spurn Head was washed away and access is on foot. It is important to observe on-site tide information. Contact Yorkshire Wildlife Trust for access details. ywt.org.uk

BEHIND HULL IS THE PLAIN OF HOLDERNESS,
LONELIER — & — LONELIER
AND AFTER THAT THE BIRDS AND LIGHTS OF SPURN HEAD, AND THEN THE SEA

Philip Larkin travelled extensively in the East Riding, regularly cycling vast distances. One of the many reasons he was fond of living in Hull was that it offered him both the city's urban environment, and also had some of East Riding's

beauty spots within reach. Larkin often visited Spurn, attracted by its scenery and the sense of freedom evoked by its remote location. Larkin's poem 'Here' depicts a sweeping journey from Hull across to Spurn.

PAST THE POPPIES BLUISH NEUTRAL DISTANCE ENDS THE LAND
SUDDENLY BEYOND A BEACH OF SHAPES AND SHINGLE

DISCOVER A POET'S LANDSCAPE   1922   No. 25/25   1985   WWW.THELARKINTRAIL.CO.UK

133

STOTT PARK BOBBIN MILL ULVERSTON

Bobbins – the wooden cylinders used to hold thread or yarn – are so small and insignificant that a tourist attraction devoted to them may seem a little odd. Their modern disappearance – replaced by plastic spools and cardboard tubes – has largely gone unnoticed. In Stott Park, however, the last working bobbin mill in Britain, the bobbin and its manufacture take pride of place. It's a window into a wonderful wooden world of Victorian industry.

Built in 1835, the mill had all the resources required for successful bobbin-making. An abundance of woodland,

where alder, ash, birch and willow trees were grown for cutting down into poles, stood alongside a plentiful supply of fast-flowing water from nearby Lake Windermere, perfect for powering the waterwheels used to drive the lathes. The thriving cloth mills of the North of England created the demand for these little wooden wonders and a ready local supply of cheap labour – with some workers as young as eight – was used to churn the bobbins out by the thousand.

Today, the mill is operated by English Heritage and entry is by guided tour. In the perfectly-preserved lathe shop,

skilled craftspeople demonstrate the bobbin-making process. The heat, noise and dust from one small bobbin is quite something. A whole workshop full must have been deafening, dangerous and dusty. The piles of woodshavings, sitting like brown snowdrifts around the machines, were used for insulation, tucked around the legs of the workers to keep them warm.

At its height, the industry supported more than 70 mills in Lakeside before the textile business sharply declined in the late 19th century. Stott Park diversified, making anything else that could be turned on a lathe, such as tool handles, table legs and toggles. Eventually more modern materials and manufacturing methods accelerated the industry's final decline, and the mill closed in 1971.

Thankfully the building's sale to the Department of Environment ensured that the mill was preserved, and it opened in 1983 to keep a little part of local history turning. The word 'bobbins' is now better known as a synonym for rubbish, but Stott Park is anything but.

ACCESS AND OPENING TIMES

Stott Park Bobbin Mill is in Colton, Ulverston, Cumbria, LA12 8AX, north of Newby Bridge off the A590. The nearest train station is at Lakeside, 11km away, where Windermere Lake Cruises from Ambleside and Bowness also stop. It is open March to October, Weds-Sun 10am-5pm. english-heritage.org.uk

THEY SHOOT HORSES, DON'T THEY? BLACKPOOL

They Shoot Horses, Don't They? is the enigmatic title of an enormous mirrorball, bringing extra sparkle to Blackpool's prom since 2002.

The 4.5-tonne ball was commissioned as part of a series of artworks designed to brighten up the redeveloped south shore and bring culture to a town seen to be lacking in it.

The perfect choice of a giant mirrorball for somewhere that hosted the long-running BBC series *Come Dancing* for many years came about almost by

accident. The artist, Michael Trainor, explains that he was trying to find 'something that could compete (visually) with the Irish Sea, the illuminations, the trams, the sky and all that seaside frenetic activity'. When he realised that he couldn't, he tried to work out how to collect everything into one easily consumable whole. The logical conclusion he came to was to make a mirrored sphere similar to a convex security mirror found in shops. For it to work on a big open space like

the prom it had to be big, and lo, the giant mirrorball was born.

For a town that never sleeps, the 46,000 mirror tiles are a perfect choice to reflect its many faces. The ball keeps turning whether it's the morning after or the night before, reflecting revellers pouring out of the nearby Pleasure Beach as it closes or morning walkers enjoying peaceful views of the Irish Sea.

Its official title, *They Shoot Horses, Don't They?*, is a nod to the 1969 film about the dance marathons of the American Depression. It's a deliberate contrast to the gaiety and sequins of Blackpool's magnificent Tower Ballroom. If it had a musical accompaniment it would be the song *Turn Turn Turn* – 'to everything there is a season'.

The mirrorball is so photogenic that it quickly became another symbol of the town, along with the tower and the trams. Its success has inspired more public art, such as the magnificent Comedy Carpet, another tribute to Blackpool's heritage as a place of entertainment and fun. Make sure you catch it to see Blackpool in a different light.

ACCESS AND OPENING TIMES
They Shoot Horses, Don't They? is part of the Great Promenade Show on New South Promenade, Blackpool, FY4 1RW.

THRELKELD QUARRY AND MINING MUSEUM THRELKELD

here are a few mining museums in the ake District to choose from, but in hrelkeld you get two attractions for the rice of one. Alongside the (very njoyable) mining museum sits the intage Excavator Trust – a peaceful lace where elderly excavators can be vingly cared for in their final days.

The trust was started by Ian Hartland, he chairman of the museum, after he iscovered a small band of engineering nthusiasts who shared his passion for scuing these amazing pieces of achinery, mainly from disused mines. he first 'Working Weekend' in 1998 roved such a success that Threlkeld ecame the epicentre of excavator

preservation, with a growing collection having ample room to roam in the grounds of the disused quarry.

There is something incongruous about these rusting vehicles set against such a beautiful natural backdrop as the Blencathra and Skiddaw fells. It's a bit like the set of a northern *Transformers* movie, with these great metal beasts waiting to spring to life and trample through the Lake District. There are tipper trucks, like giant Tonka toys, and excavators with huge scoops, ready to pick you up. The daddy of them all is 'King Kong' with a scoop so large a whole family can comfortably fit inside with room for a picnic.

139

The mining museum itself is also worth visiting, with geological displays, mining exhibits, mineral panning and a narrow gauge steam railway. If you have time to take the mine tour, a short meander through the mine makes it clear what a difficult, thankless job miners had. A dangerous occupation, working in semi-darkness, full of noise and dust, it wasn't for the faint-hearted. Modern visits are more fun. Children get to ride in the mine cart, a nice change from a rollercoaster, and to blow out the candle on a miner's helmet to experience total darkness, a rarity these days. They can also learn how to tell

talactites from stalagmites, all about
oreholes, and vibration whitefinger,
nd how smoking was used as a way of
reventing disease. All in all it's a
mashing day out.

ACCESS AND OPENING TIMES
Threlkeld Quarry is situated opposite the
village of Threlkeld, 5km east of Keswick
on the A66, CA12 4TT. It is open daily
from Easter to October, 10am-5pm.
threlkeldquarryandminingmuseum.co.uk

THE TOAST RACK MANCHESTER

If you ask directions to Manchester Metropolitan University's former Hollings Campus you might get some blank looks, but if you ask for the Toast Rack everyone will know what you mean.

Once you catch sight of it there's no need to explain its nickname – it's a huge tapering building with parabolic concrete arches on top that give it the look of a great big toastrack. There is a story that in the 1970s students made a giant slice of polystyrene toast and stuck it on the roof for rag week. And if that wasn't enough, to augment the big breakfast theme there is an adjoining building which being small and round is known as The Poached Egg.

The culinary moniker fits well as the building, described by architectural historian Sir Nikolaus Pevsner as 'a perfect piece of pop architecture', began life as a classroom block for Manchester's Domestic and Trades College where cookery and domestic science was taught. It was later home to MMU's Faculty of Food, Clothing and Hospitality.

Management, known as Hollings Campus after its redoubtable principal Elsie Hollings.

The buildings were designed in 1958 by City Architect L C (Leonard) Howitt who was also responsible for re-modelling the interior of Manchester Free Trade Hall and designing the Crown Court in Crown Square. Although the design is playful, it is practical too. The tapering shape provided different-sized teaching spaces for small or large classes and the adjoining buildings provided space for noisy tailoring workshops and central facilities.

Grade II listed in 1998 it is one of the great moments of postwar architecture, embodying the spirit of optimism and ingenuity that prevailed in the late 1950s. The building is not to everyone's taste, but many have grown to love it. When the university announced that they would be vacating the premises in 2013, the Manchester Modernist Society moved in to delve into its archives and celebrate its starring role in the city's skyline. It was put up for sale in 2014 and will hopefully pop up with a new lease of life sometime soon.

ACCESS AND OPENING TIMES
The Toast Rack is at Hollings Campus, Manchester, M14 6HR.
thetoastrack.wordpress.com

TYNE PEDESTRIAN AND CYCLIST TUNNELS HOWDON AND JARROW

Opened in 1951, the Tyne Pedestrian and Cyclist Tunnels join the communities of Howdon and Jarrow on the north and south banks of the River Tyne. The purpose-built Cycle Tunnel was the first of its kind in Britain, meaning two legs or two wheels were equally good. They were Grade II listed in 2000 and are currently undergoing extensive refurbishment to conserve their history and make them suitable for 21st-century travel.

At their peak 20,000 people travelled 274m through them each day to get to work in the local shipyards. As it's a public highway, the tunnels will continue to be free and open 24 hours a day. Entry is through a dinky red-brick rotunda at each end, which is quiet apart from the faint whirr and clank of machinery.

For more than 50 years, the journey to the tunnels has been via two 60m wooden escalators – magnificent things, designed by Waygood Otis. When they were built, they were the longest single-rise escalators in the world. Today they are still the longest wooden ones in the world. Sadly, as amazing as they are, they have reached the end of their natural life and are soon to be replaced by an inclined lift, although one on each end will be kept for posterity and

illuminated with feature lighting when the refurbishment ends in summer 2015.

After the graceful ride to the bottom there's something incredibly beautiful about the twin tunnel entrances, signposted in elegant 1950's lettering. Although they look identical the cycle tunnel is slightly wider. Both are resplendent in cool cream and green tiles, giving an undersea air. Tunnels can be dank and smelly, but this pair are cool and spotless. At the halfway point, the divide between the counties of Durham and Northumberland is marked in blue lettering, so a simple walk or cycle to work feels like a cross-border expedition.

ACCESS AND OPENING TIMES
The north entrance is just off Bewicke Street (A187). It is signposted from the main road. The south is at Tyne Street, Jarrow, off the A19.
tynepedestrianandcyclisttunnels.co.uk

← **CYCLISTS TUNNEL**

DANGER Limited overhead height

PEDESTRIANS TUNNEL →

NOTICE NO CYCLING ALLOWED AT ALL!

SECURITY NOTICE

CYCLISTS THIS WAY

EMAS

COUNTY OF NORTHUMBERLAND

WHITELEYS BRIDLINGTON

Standing proud on Bridlington's Promenade, Ernest Whiteley & Co has been clothing the good ladies of East Yorkshire for more than 100 years. As the artfully arranged shop windows draw you in, time seems to stand still. Immaculately-dressed mannequins welcome you to a cosy world of flannelette and net curtains, doilies and rain bonnets – now so old-fashioned that it seems impossibly foreign.

Through the carefully laid-out (and wheelchair-friendly) shop, there are handkerchiefs, gloves, swimming costumes, vests, pants, fearsome-looking bras, socks, suspenders, bath mats, sewing things, dresses, tea towels and dusters. Everything has its place in the perfectly preserved shop-fittings.

This is the sort of store where style never goes out of fashion, and the change of season has little effect – a practical move for the unpredictable British climate. The thermals are out in July and the swimming costumes are still here in December. Likewise, there is no body fascism here – big sizes are the norm and everyone is catered for. It's a refreshing sight.

Among the many familiar items there

are those that are now harder to find – antimacassars, garters, rain bonnets and corsets. There is something very Alan Bennett about the whole scene. As closing time nears, sunlight strafes across the tabards, illuminating the new season's net curtains. The uninhabited clothes, wrapped in a warm fug of nostalgia, are like characters waiting to come to life.

Staffed by mature ladies, the Whiteleys slogan is 'We care with a chair'. There's no rush here, and no hard sell. It is a family business through and through – Ann Clough, the founder's grand-daughter has worked in the shop for more than 50 years and still loves every minute of it. She should have retired years ago, but can't bear to leave.

In the decades since she started here there have been changes, but Whiteleys secret is not messing with classic, practical products. Their top-selling range is 'sensible underwear for older ladies'. With patrons in their 80s, 90s and beyond, Whiteleys is catering for a customer that the high street has forgotten. It's a real retail rarity.

ACCESS AND OPENING TIMES
Whiteleys is at 67 Promenade, Bridlington town centre, YO15 2QE. It is closed on Thursdays and Sundays.

151

WITHERNSEA
LIGHTHOUSE MUSEUM WITHERNSEA

Withernsea Lighthouse is not your average lighthouse. Poking up 38m from a row of houses in Hull Road, the bright white octagonal tower looks like it might have been blown inland or tossed there by a passing wave.

Built in 1894 because of the high number of shipwrecks on this stretch of coast, its lamp shone for 27km until modern navigational technology made obsolete in 1976. Now it serves as a loc history museum with the flotsam and

jetsam of Withernsea and its citizens pleasantly jumbled around the base of the lighthouse and adjoining lighthouse keepers' cottages.

There are few buildings as distinctive and delightful as lighthouses, so enjoy the beautiful sight of the spiral staircase that curves round its hollow core to the top. The dizzying climb of 144 steps is all worth it when you emerge from the narrow ladder into the lantern room. Unusually the first things you see are rooftops and back gardens as the lighthouse is almost 1km inland – since this part of the coast is prone to coastal erosion, that was the only safe place to put it.

On the way back down, stop and admire the collection of old lightbulbs and model boats. Nautical flags adorn the staircase and the bottom of the tower has a pleasantly salty collection of RNLI and fishing memorabilia – knots, lifebelts, and mannequins kitted out in oilskins and sou'westers ready for life on the ocean wave.

In the old lighthouse keepers' cottages, the roar of the crowd drowns out the roar of the sea with a shrine to local lass, Kay Kendall, who made her way from Hull Road to Hollywood. Born a few houses away in 1926, she had various acting roles before making her name with *Genevieve* in 1953. The small but evocative display celebrates her early life in Withernsea, her shining career on the silver screen and marriage to Rex Harrison before her premature death in 1959.

After this little taste of glitz, refresh yourself in the excellent tearoom and enjoy the beautiful garden. Lighthouses are often about austerity and solitude, but this one combines the smell of the sea with the heart of the town and a whiff of glamour.

ACCESS AND OPENING TIMES

Withernsea Lighthouse is on Hull Road, Withernsea, East Yorkshire, HU19 2DY. It is open on weekend afternoons from Easter to October with additional weekday opening during school summer holidays. withernsealighthouse.co.uk

A WORLD IN MINIATURE CARLISLE

In the basement of Houghton Hall Garden Centre in Carlisle is A World in Miniature. This superb collection goes beyond the ordinary boundaries of scale modelling with more than 50 exquisitely-detailed model shops, gardens and household scenes made in incredible detail by some of the world's leading miniature makers. The artistry and skill that goes into this is amazing, never mind the patience and eyesight.

Everything here is made to an exacting 1/12 scale, with every detail from the original shrunk down to minute size, whether it's perfectly woven rugs, tiny marquetry, intricate Petit Point needlework or hand-blown glass goblets.

As well as being beautifully made, the displays are warm and humorous, with little touches that could really make you believe that a race of tiny humans lived here. A minuscule glass of wine sits on a side table, a teeny Toby jug looks down from a weeny bookcase, and the smallest

pair of spectacles you've ever seen rests casually on a miniature chest of drawers.

The biographies of the makers, many of them members of the International Guild of Miniature Artisans, show that this is a craft, not a hobby. The Chinese cabinet by 'The Master' John Hodgson is a sight to behold. The detail, which would be noteworthy at full size, is breath-taking in miniature. In the Library, created by the late Anne Greatrix,

each of the 445 books is hand-bound.

This small world is one of the finest collections of its kind. A magnifying glass is included in the entrance fee so you won't miss anything.

ACCESS AND OPENING TIMES
A World in Miniature Museum is at Houghton Hall Garden Centre, Houghton, Carlisle, Cumbria, CA6 4JB. It is open from Monday to Saturday, 10am to 5pm, and on Sunday from 10am to 3.30pm. aworldinminiature.com

SOURCES

Couple: Sean Henry – An Offshore Sculpture, Inspire Northumberland, 2008
A Guide to Port Sunlight Village by Edward Hubbard and Michael Shippobottom, Liverpool University Press, 2nd ed 2005
100 Years at Shipley Glen: The Story of the Glen Tramway, M.J.Leak
Food on the Move: the Extraordinary World of the Motorway Service Area by David Lawrence, Alain de Botton, Laurie Taylor and Sancha Briffa, 2010
nothingtoseehere.net